ALL THOSE SILENCES AROUND ME...

MAALU

Copyright © Maalu
All Rights Reserved.

For the 12-year-old former self who never gave up on her dreams...

Contents

Contents

Contents

1. Dying Young Beside A Cradle...

I hear a voice...
So angelic it seems to me...
So soft and tender...
So soothing and sweet...
I've imagined her to be beautiful...
Even though she's not pretty...
Her heartbeat I can hear...
A lullaby to my ears...
How I wished to see her...
How I wished to kiss her...
How I wished to fight with her...
How I wished to kiss her sorry...
I counted the days...
Going by all along...
Impatient to meet her...
My mother oh my mother...
My mother would've knitted me a sweater...
Oh...! She must've made something tasty...
My mother knows I love pink...
And she's happy I can feel...
My mother must be buying me hats...
And the tiny little socks for my feet...
And all the tender clothes with fragrance...
That is always sweeter than any flower...

She must be telling my father...
That I'm going to come sooner or later...
That they need one tiny pink room...
For my young little cradle where I shall sleep...
But life's not easy as I say...
I'm a girl... she knows now...
Oh...! She doesn't want me now...
She hates me now...
I'm sorry I'm a girl...
But I still want to see you...
And kiss on your cheek...
And get wrapped up in your arms...
But you don't love me now...
You don't want me now...
How to weep now...
My tears might be a curse to you...
I would not cry...
I would not hate...
For all these can be a curse to you...
Which I can't gift you... my mother...
I still count my days painfully...
For your wellbeing...
And the days crept in...
And I breathe my last breath beside a cradle...

2. The Eight Year Old...

I can't sing anymore...
(I'm calling out to rapists with my sound)
I can't dance anymore...
(I'm drawing their attention with my curves)
I can't walk outside...
(I would be raped by someone who believes night is danger)
I can't wear short clothes...
(I'd be stared till I regret my choice)
I can't be a rebel anymore...
(My kids will be raped one day)
And... I can't pray anymore...
(I'll be raped soon after the rituals)
#justiceforasifa

3. Bleeding Words...

She sat at her desk with a pen...
And a bottle of ink that was new...
Her glasses fixed upon her nose...
And her head full of thoughts...
Memories haunting...
And the future ridiculing...
The chaos forming up around...
Like the swirling hurricane...
Drawing her further in...
The nib drenched the sheets...
That were centuries old...
Golden and crumbled...
And the edges torn...
She filled in those papers...
The pain she'd been hiding...
Her fears of her childhood...
And the nightmares that had followed...
Whispers were louder...
And so were the howls...
Every bit she wrote...
Took up ink from her heart...
She might think how Umbridge seemed better...
For she only made Harry bleed on his hand...
But life seemed much cruel...
For life bled her heart...

4. I Sit On My Bed...

I sit on my bed...
Staring at the mirror...
I see no smiles...
I see no tears...
But I do see a crack...
A crack in my skull...
And something fell out...
Something metal... a screw...
And something else followed...
Also metal...
Six hard nuts...
They bounced from that crack...
One by one in discipline...
They bounced off my skull..
Over to my collarbone...
They rolled down my breast...
And bounced over my thigh...
And finally they fell on the white marble tiles...
With a ringing sound so loud...
I still see no smiles...
I still see no tears...
I tried to see if I could feel anything in my flesh...
But nothing did make sense anymore...
My stomach didn't growl...
The beast has finally died...

My chest didn't ache anymore...
My heart stopped beating...
My skin stuck to my bones...
And my cheeks sunk in deeper...
A hollowed mask of despair and grief...
I shrank so much...
My limbs...
My tummy...
Everything shrank...
And my back curled...
I became a hunchback dwarf...
My distorted mechanic body fell backwards...
My cracked skull hit the pillows...
Like in a slow motion movie...
I see myself falling...
I see the pillows shrink...
And my head gently bounced...
In the distance all I heard...
I guess...
A boy must've blew a yellow balloon...
Till it burst on his face...
And it bled his lip...
And scarred his heart with fear...
The burst was loud...
I could hear...
The boy stared at his own invisible breath before...
Now he see...
He had wasted his breath for nothing...
And so one might think...

"I've wasted so much of my pure love on her...

But she died anyway...

She killed herself...

I've simply wasted my love...

I've wasted it on her...

I could've spent it on...

Someone else..."

5. There...

There... on that branch...
Is a crow staring at the sky...
Alone with his mates...
Alone with his wits...
He crowed at the bright shining orb...
That lit the dark shy...
And crowed again... and yet again...
Until he told me...
The contents of a sealed message...
His eyes had fire... orange flames of Hell...
Here he's in this land...
Crowing in his imbecile cries...
The message... oh... I nearly forgot...
Was sealed in black... with an emblem...
Oh... the emblem of two horns...
Lord Yama I assume...
It's time... that fateful truth...
Everlasting since time immemorial...
The sentence to my trials...
I've proved wrong... proved guilty...
Proved guilty with facts in His court...
With no mercy at His hand...
Dry eyed crow... from where he came...
There's not enough moist...
No beautiful rivers...

Nor any spongy mossy rocks...

He crowed again... asked me to follow his wings...

Oh... how wretched of a life I've...

No wings... no winds to aid...

The seal burnt in my palms...

My pale palms blackened in ash...

His cries pierced my ears...

As I dangle from the white ceiling fan...

Oh no... did I forget to confess...

The confession of how I murdered myself...?

Yes... I hung myself from the ceiling...

I was a pretty decoration to my house...

A pretty showcase doll to exhibit...

In pretty yellow clothes...

And pretty red lipstick...

I looked like a doll they said...

A darling doll...

They forget I was no Barbie...

With a perfect plastic life...

Who stood silently...

Letting them strip me naked to the core...

But I was Anabelle... devilish Anabelle...

Who murdered her enemies in sleep...

Oh no... but my time has come...

Time to depart...

Oh... I hope my soul rests in peace...

But if you mortals are lucky...

You'll see my strolling late at night...

With big white flowers I my hair...

That tempt you into my traps...
That be purified in your blood...

6. His Paper Planes...

those pebbles rolled down...
the depths of the river took them with her flow...
far far away i see a paper plane...
aimed at the crown of my golden leaves...
would it make any sense... little one...
when those get stuck in my branches..?
will it ever give you those answers...
that you'd been looking for so long in your life...?
he said nothing... but smiled...
he'd lost his favourite kite in me...
few paper planes would never harm...
why... those were just some paper planes after all...
now my crown has become green...
a tender freshness in every leaf of mine...
i saw him again... with paper planes...
bigger ones he'd now...
he was tall now...
and his hair in coils...
his eyes were like orbs...
of molten gold from sun...
he was angry... angry for something...
he rushed towards me and threw those paper planes...
one by one... all those stuck in my crown...
indeed they bleed with his confessions...
that he told no one else...

now my crown has become dull...
with little leaves and even little fruits...
he stood afar...
no more of those paper planes that i missed...
no more gestures of hurt...
he got taller again...
with longer hair...
his face showed nothing...
nor it gave away tears...
the saw went through me... just above my roots...
no... it didn't hurt me a bit...
it didn't hurt me at all when i fell...
oh yes... but it did hurt me a bit...
when he took those paper planes off my crown...
one by one... he took out those poems he once wrote...
that i... a tree failed to read...
a tear dropped down from his eyes...
those orbs made of molten gold...
none of his words had died...
in wind... rain... or even heat...
he pressed his palm on my branches...
i felt them burning me down...
i never thought that sun could weep...
these silver threads that he stole from the moon...
i smiled as i closed my eyes...
feeling his palms leave my branches for the last...
he never saw my roots that stayed...
maybe he'll see me when i'm reborn...

7. No... Not Peace... No More Of That Illusion...

"AAAAAAAAAAAAAAAAAARGH..."

The silence was broken... peace left...

And then it grew again... the silence...

No... not peace... no more of that illusion...

The darker it got... more silent it became...

No... not peace... no more of that illusion...

More screams were heard... more wailings...

More of the cries that terrorised the silences...

No... not peace... no more of that illusion...

No more wolves howled nor the moon shone...

And still myths had it... a wild spirit crying out...

The silence grew again...

No... not peace... no more of that illusion...

But terrifying silences of the dark...

Faded drumbeats are heard... no not drums...

Heart... scared... frightened hearts...

Silences had its share of frights...

Bless the soul... temple bells scream at midnight...

Those stony labyrinths lost their sense of their time...

The temple bells screamed at the top of their stony lungs...

"AAAAAAAAAAAAAAAAAAAAAARGH..."

More screams... more silences....

The temple bells began in the middle... her endings lost...

Fiery chill crept through the dark...

Hide now... pretend you've slept...

Close your eyes... pretend you've slept...

The silence grew again...

No... not peace... no more of that illusion...

Hide safe... under this purple blanket...

Sleep now... my frightened children...

Those shadows glide away...

They won't hurt sleeping children...

Sleeping children are invisible...

"AAAAAAAAAAAAAAAAAARGH..."

The screams are louder... the shadows nearer...

The temple bells scream somewhere in the distant...

Somewhere far...

The fiery chills intensifies... and I watch...

The scared faces of my children...

The silence grew louder...

No... not peace... no more of that illusion...

The barriers within us and the chaos... lit in orange flames...

I swear I saw two wings... sharp like razor blades...

It's just a dream so real... just a nightmare...

My little children... you;ll wake up soon...

Sleep now... hide under this purple blanket...

Sleeping children are invisible...

They won't hurt sleeping babies...

As our shadow rose to the darkened skies...

I watched the scared faces of my little ones...

Following me to a reality beyond this nightmare...

The silence screamed louder...

No... not peace... no more of that illusion...

8. Burn My Temples...

"Burn my temples...
And drown my idols..."
Cried He with a voice so loud...
As the thunder above...
"Pluck out...
Those golden eyes of mine...
I... your God commands you...
Obey me or burn yourself..."
"I'm ashamed of you...
The wrath you behold...
You judge your myths too much...
You don't see the morals..."
"You've worshipped the characters...
You forgot to see Me...
I... your God...
Has died for you..."
"Burn your idols now...
I don't need you to save me...
You mock your fellow dears...
With devotion that has dried..."
"I see green, orange and white...
In a war for Me it seems...
You forget that I'm a rainbow...
All my names constitute one..."
"Stop it... stop it now I say...

I don't want to see this madness...
You pray to Me for peace...
Whom would I cry for My mistakes...
I've created... for I've no escape from them..."

9. Haunting Pasts...

Her curves tempted me...
That serpent head... that little witch...
She'd charmed me with her smiles...
And now her lips talk...
They talk if stories... dried up past...
Drowned in mind's little games...
Of gains and losses...
Of grey dice rolling...
Of all the turn of events...
She imprisoned me...
Chained me to her voice...
Caramalised and smooth as silk...
The past that's least spoken of...
Least brought on top...
She was merciless tonight...
Spoke only of losses...
The turn of events...
Those dice had predicted...
The turn of events least expected...
She took me down the roads...
Which led to her past...
Crooked little paths...
Narrowed down to very few lines...
She made me walk hand in hand...
Met characters that held a role...

Some distant role perhaps...
I've never known them...
Nor will I ever learn who they're...
Some where old...
With grey hairs and wrinkled skin...
Some where young...
With knowledge of past unrolled...
Those that we met... kept staring at me...
Wondering who this new face was...
Wondering who this intruder was...
Wondering how I time travelled back...
There were houses down the roads...
White and green... white and brown...
And an ancient mansion too...
That looked like it had more stories to sing...
There were lost fields and river stories...
Like the lost city of Atlantis...
Of the time when people talked...
Of times people feared nothing but death...
Stories of broken hearts...
Of confused hearts...
Of stories that breathed life...
That had sudden attacks...
The dice kept rolling...
The numbers appeared with every roll...
1... 2... 3... 4... 5... 6...
Numbers made their way with every roll...
There were forked roads...
Every tempting path was wrong...

How do I know...?
I just guess...
"All that glitters isn't gold..."
I saw... stories no one told me...
I lived through somebody else's past...
Somebody who was much older than me...
Somebody who's seen a lot in life...
And when that final road...
Has been chosen and pursued...
That temptress...
That time traveller...
She'd vanished into thin air...
Leaving me alone in darkened path...
Every stories buried once again...
Every past drowned in mind's little games...
Every failures cherished with survivals...
Every brightened details once again masked...
Some stories are like her...
A temptress that tempts...
A serpent head with secrets...
A burnt heart with scarlet scars...
I look back once again...
The roads that curve back...
That roads that I've come through...
And I feel...
I feel pride...
Pride that there's always a smile...
And a heart that never gives up...
And that's all that matters...

10. Little Rubber Duck...

I see... in the middle of that ocean...

A yellow rubber duck floating...

Solitary and carelessly...

The anchor not dropping to depths...

It floats away...

The white waves carrying it...

And its aim so lost... so uncertain...

The boats sailed past the rubber duck...

No one heard its tiny squeak...

No one noticed that anchor on its hat...

No one saw it so lost...

Boats passed by... one by one...

Dragging weights unwillingly behind...

Their heavy anchors made them slow...

Unlike the little one...

The little rubber took along...

An ebony boat passed by...

With skeletal scaveners rowing...

A little scavenger girl saw the solitary one...

The little rubber duck that float along...

She poured black oil around...

Hoping she could drown...

The solitary rubber duck to the depths...

To be long forgotten in those curses...

But the rubber duck slipped and drifted...

Drifted far away and did not drown...
Did not give up... not yet...
The oil however lost its fight...
The little scavenger girls growled...
And threw the barrel afloat...
Took out a match and struck the light...
The sea catching orange fires...
The rubber duck drifted apart...
Once again escaped all the perils...
Drifted far far away...
And the little scavenger girl lost her game...

11. Have You Ever Looked At A Mirror...

Have you ever looked at a mirror...
For too long...
No... not to comb your hair...
Nor to put some Kajal...
Nor to count your pimples...
Nor to curl your eyelashes...
Nor to spike up your moustache...
But to see the little child...
That little face filled with scars...
Scarlet scars of injustice...
In a criss-cross upon her rosy cheeks...
Looking back at you with teary eyes...
With a crouched spine full of fears...
A little child who has been denied her justice...?
Have you ever looked at a mirror...
For too long...
And wondered why that reflection...
Looks strangely unfamiliar but familiar...
That teary eyes seeming to tell a story...
Of those criss-cross scars...
Of haunting scarlet pasts...
And wondered why your past...
Isn't a black and white film...
Played onscreen in repeat...

As they're for your fellow mates...?
Have you ever looked at a mirror...
For too long...
And wondered why...
Your mother instincts wouldn't help...
That little girl in your mirror...
To heal her fresh and deepening scars...
That doesn't look like they would heal...
Even after her pitiful death...?
Have you ever looked at a mirror...
For too long...
And watched your past rewind and play...
On repeat in different speeds...
And still feel what you felt then...
That wouldn't change...
Even after so many years...
Even when the scars kept deepening still...
Until you're sure they would split you...
Not just in half... but in millions and billions...
And all you could is to watch again...
Repeat after repeat...
Hurting harder still...?
Have you ever looked at a mirror...
For too long...
Have you felt sad for that little one...
Because you couldn't help her get up...
From her broken knees...
And dirty torn clothes...
And her dishevelled hair...

And not able to adopt her...
To love her and care for her...
Just as she deserves to be...?
Oh... if I keep asking questions...
I would never stop...
And you would run out of answers...
You'll bend your knees...
And fold your hands before me...
And accept defeat...
Because I'm one of those little girls...
In that reflection you see...
Who had been wronged by fate...
And denied justice...
The only difference...
Is that my right is your left...
And my left is your right...

12. A Witch's Treasure...

There was a castle...

Where I was born...

Not a gigantic one...

But bigger that any I've seen yet...

There was a secret room round the corner...

To where only I'd access to...

A room beyond "Open Sesame..."

But quite the same...

There were ancient books...

With yellow crumbling pages...

Breathing painfully hard...

Begging me to let out their secrets...

That were stacked quite so neat...

One book after another...

Where all the worlds collapsed into an empire...

I could conjure myself into any world...

Unlike being called to by Aslan...

Or I could even keep my emotions stacked up high...

Like a horcrux out of reach...

From Muggle eyes...

I stole myself into that room every night...

When every other mortal fell asleep...

After day's hard-working...

Snoring and drooling on their pillow covers...

Stingy after their night's endeavours...

Cuddling under soft pinkish blankets...

I always looked like one of those little girls...

That we all have met once or twice in Western horror movies...

Holding up a lamp that might go off in a wind...

With the most softest hair that even ghouls fall in love with...

And with a fear that crept upon my face...

That was quite natural for me to have...

Under one of these darkest nights...

I loved pressing my ears to the walls...

Trying to remember where the secret gap was...

Where a golden lever stood...

Which when pulled down gives an ancient key...

(I was a tougher detective...

Not even Indiana Jones could pull it off...)

But that night was quite unfortunate...

The key went missing...

And it panicked me more than it should...

Bringing tears into my brown eyes...

I kept my oil lamp on the stony floor...

And pulled my hair tightly... back into a bun...

And kept pulling the lever hard...

Hoping to find the key stuck somewhere...

Suddenly there came an eerie sound from behind...

I stood still... forgetting to breathe...

I could feel drops of perspiration...

13. Man's Bestfriend...

Somewhere far... howls that wretched bitch...

Under the silver moonlight...

That shines desperately...

Through the darkening clouds...

Her howls bring forth pain...

Suffering.. I believe... a repeated mourning...

She's lost... lost forever... something... or someone...

That bloodcurdling howl...

Pierces every living ear around...

Hark... every howl is growing feeble...

A soft but trembling terrifying howl...

Her breath spreads in that cold airs of the dark night...

Embracing every life as it floats...

And tumble on every possible hurdle in its path...

Touching lightly... a feather touch...

And moves and moves...

And floats and floats...

Until her very last breath...

Becomes warm air...

That is chilled by moonlit night...

A knife on her shoulder...

Pierced deep enough for her death...

But not deep enough for her easy sudden death...

Every pain... she'd to watch and feel...

And batter her heart before her departure...

Her hind leg was in distorted angle...
And she limped with her three good ones...
Made it to those little pups...
Before Death could grasp her by her neck...
Two fine bitches they were...
Beauties like their mother... one would say...
Who lied silent... still...
With blood running between their hind legs...
And their throats slit open...
Like those great chasms into fiery hell beneath...
Their three tiny brothers were stolen...
And she'd tried... tried hard to save them...
And their sisters died in failed attempts...
And their mother... wounded to death...
One more pack... no... one more family of stray dogs...
Lie numb beneath the starry moonlight...
Her painful howls died...
With a silent whimper at the end...
A silent protest of hers...
A silent sing-song of hers...
Stray dogs... they were just stray dogs...
The ones without red, yellow, green or black collars...
Without chains and bars to cage them...
I say... they're more lucky than she...
And her sons have been stolen for such a future...
Caged they maybe... they'll survive still... they'll live...
Oh... if they could speak...
They would share their childhood traumas...
Their journey to become "man's best friend..."

14. A Random Memory...

A random memory...
A fragment from the past... a blurred past...
Red in colour... smudged and slimy...
Thousand needles at one point... at heart...
Bulging eyes... dark circles... red puffy eyes...
But lips curved towards eyes... the corners...
Like those lovers... eager to meet... after centuries...
A smile... fake than plastic flowers... imitating someone...
Wide smile... not letting go of the dark secret...
What the dark night witnessed...
The pillows drenched... and cold... stormy in monsoon nights...
The familiar salty taste linger... the musty scent persists...
Stained walls and broken floor...
The bed creaks...
She yells from behind the locked door...
The bed creaks louder...
The chilly breeze crawl through the cracked windows...
The curtains dance... like dull belly dancers...
Out of shape... out of routine... out of monotony...
A hope of warm breath fills the stony room... the last breath...
A ray of hope... extinguished...
Like a helpless flame exposed in storm...
The room grows colder...
Her screams louder from behind the locked door...
The victim... the dark figure... grew colder still...

The flame died... the hope left...

A random memory it was...

Five years ago she was alive...

Five years from then... she's a fragment from past...

15. Road to Storm...

Every storm breaks loose...
Every breath escapes...
A praise wouldn't make me smile...
A slap wouldn't make me silent...
A blackmail wouldn't make me afraid...
I've seen too much... felt too much...
The trauma lingers behind...
Like one of those shadows of the past...
How powerful past can be...!!!
The strings break open...
The threads splits open...
Last hope too vanish...
Future hangs before as mirage...
From clouds of terrible despair and gloom...
Those roads lead straight to storm...
That stayed silent beneath my skin...
That shook and trembled only my veins...
That screamed from deep within...
Terrible pain lingers...
No marks... no scars... no rash...
Nothing that's visible to naked eye persists...
Back curved down and knees bent...
A leash on the neck and voices to lead...
Tears would never let go...
Lips would never split open...

Throat would never tremble...
Not even a single sigh would escape...
That's what they said it tastes like...
That metallic taste of trauma...
That metallic taste of anger...
Yes... yes... it had a taste...
That metallic taste...
That lingers on your tongue when you go sick...
That same metallic taste...
That murders your taste buds...
And it lingered... that same taste...
Lingered on my lips too...
That murdered every tastes I had...
A trance of paralysis...
That's what the taste made me...
A dreadful diety it was...
With a baby face and burning red eyes...
A mask to lure all into trap...
It stays... it lingers... it hangs by my throat...
Ther's no escape... no runaways...
It follows... that fool's mask...
That past... that trauma...
And I've to deal...
That darkness that makes me... me...
That past that makes me... me...
And then...
It all sounds mad...
When the silence around me gets loud...
For I'm this... this cyclone...

And none can love me for who I'm...

16. Words Spill Out...

Words spill out...
Like waterfalls...
When the silence spreads...
When the blood flows from veins...
Blade cut veins...
With a silence that came from within...
An owl screams outside...
A bat circles the moon...
A dog howls and others join...
Cats fight over who gets food tonight...
The water goes splash over the wound...
Bloody little bucket and bathroom...
Bloodied mind and body...
Blood of an unknown impurity...
Few days before...
He was out on streets singing...
He was all about buying new toys...
A little over twelve maybe...
With heart full of colours for the world...
"What do you lack...?
You've food, home and parents...
You've clothes and friends and life...
You're not crippled or mentally retarded...
You're living a life others crave for...
What more do you need...?

You've got everything...
Still you say you're depressed...
Aren't you ashamed...?"
He had walked around...
As if he was the happiest child ever...
But on an unfortunate morning...
He was raped by his own elders...
Whom he was taught to respect...
He cried aloud in muted screams...
His tears echoed far and wide...
Some secrets were meant to be kept...
Boys cannot get raped... only girls could...
And boys don't cry... only girls would...
He tried speaking up...
But he was impure...
He felt the doors of temples and mosques...
Closing down infront of him...
Barring him from the entry...
He cut his vein...
He watched the blood ooze out...
He'd red blood...
And so did the pure ones too...
He was pure enough...
He smiled...
He would be let into the heaven...
And would sit on the lap of God...
He closed his eyes with a smile...
And let Death take him in His chariot...
How many more like this you say...?

Wasting away because of negligence...
A psycho... they all called him...
Only he knew of his normal real life...

17. What If...?

What if...
I decide to leave you...
Finally...
When I'd someone to understand me...?
What if...
I let you go...
Watch you walk away...
With blurred eyes and running nose...
With pain that breaks my heart...
And still don't stop you...
And still let you walk away...?
What if...
I scream my heart out...
Confessing that I'll never be free...
From my insanity and my fears...
Finally...
Accepting that brutal truth...
Unable to keep people around me...
Because I keep pushing them away...
When they finally understand me...?
What if...
You hear all my screams...
And stick on to me...
Like paper on glue...
To separate us...

Would be like tearing apart...
A brutal pain...
We cannot run away from...?
What if...
I keep pushing you away...
Knowing that I'm tearing us apart...
And still keep on doing...
Like a psychotic on streets...
Roaming under dim streetlights...
Looking for fresh blood to spill...?
What if...
I stab you from behind...
With knife that's metaphor...
And make you bleed...
That too a metaphor...
And watch you drown...
Again a metaphor...
Like I'm made of metaphors...
And I myself is a metaphor...?
What if...?
Finally...
You realise that I'm just a metaphor...
And that I don't exist...
That I was a fragment...
Of your fragmented dreams...
A shadow from your past...?
What if...
You really really walk away...
And I linger longingly...

Under those dimmed streetlights...
Clutching onto my hair...
And tearing them off...
One by one...
All down to streets...?

18. Search...

We search...
We search for a lot of things...
A lot of meanings...
We go behind a lot of lines...
Green and red and black discontinuous...
That run up and down entangled in embraces...
In every map that the world simply gives us...
Under the blue sky... under the black sky...
Under the sun... under the moon and stars...
Under that simple north star who gleams...
Under every conspiring universe...
Strewn in metaphors and oxymorons...
We search and search blindly...
For something that we always wanted...
Some of us have a word...
Some of us have a clue...
Some of us know the paths...
But the destiny always makes us wonder...
Was it this that we'd searched for...?
"After all this time...?
Always..."

19. My Little Trauma Child...

Everything's dark nowadays...

And my diary is crammed with poetry...

Of every stained nightmares...

That spills from my silver nib...

I conceal myself within four walls...

Like a treasure out of reach of pirates...

My fan spins a hundred in a single puff...

That storm muffling my screams...

Past does haunt...

Like being pushed into fathomless depths...

A burial it's... of some sorts...

Buried with a stone weighing me down...

My eyes feel heavy and saggy...

I can't feel them any longer...

My whole flesh and blood frozen...

Under my loyal pet of a fan...

I've dreamt last night...

Of two beautiful dancers in red and gold...

Ready to dance before the gods...

When the whole world was in sleeping wake...

They screamed as they ran out...

Terrified of the phantom they saw...

The temple almost in debris...

Still had its last surviving breaths...

The breath smelled of rotten gas...
Something shone afar dimly...
Under the clouded skies... .
There were phantoms of injustice...
Floating in silence...
Led by a little girl...
Her clothes ripped open...
And her skin almost falling off...
Greenish skin and pale eyes...
Her breath stinking of rotten flesh...
She walked towards me...
(Those dancers were long gone...)
I couldn't move a single muscle...
She held me frozen with her glance...
She tilted her tiny head...
Must've been a pretty lady once...
Her eyes looked past me...
As if she was performing my autopsy
Before those gods who were witnesses...
"How could phantoms survive with gods...?
Gods killed phantoms, wasn't that the rule...?
Why... why... why...?
Was I going crazy between fantasy and reality...?"
My doubts never found voice...
"We weren't safe when we lived..."
She said as if she read my thoughts...
"We... phantoms of injustice...
We speak of prophecies and downfalls...
For we faced all that when we lived...

But remember who I'm...?

I'm not simply a phantom of injustice...

I'm a phantom of your fears...

I'm your phantom in underworld...

You denied me proper burial...

You denied me justice...

You stripped off my dignity...

And you claim a survivor over my corpse..."

"I did no injustice to you...

I buried you because I was afraid...

I was afraid of the trauma...

That would eventually haunt me to my pyre..."

Somehow my voice bounced off my vocal cords...

"I know... you were a child...

But you're a grown up young woman now...

Your fear only gave you away to your trauma...

It's time you give me my justice...

And release yourself from this pain...

Let me rest in peace at last..."

The next day... everything was fine...

I buried her safely as she had instructed...

Day by day... month by month... year by year...

Slow but progressive steps...

I shall come to peace some day...

That poor little girl was my past...

I hugged her close to my chest...

When no other human could tolerate her odour...

Nor to remain brave in her presence...

20. Hoax...

I think my darkness is a hoax...
Darker as the time moves
In trembling concentric circles...
History repeating again and again...
But always apart from the core...
I think my fears are a hoax too...
A big black joke played at me...
A gigantic illusion that haunts my sense...
Until I quit and run away from these lights...
That's filled with black and white extremes...
Silent whispers were part of it...
This hoax that dives...
Right from those black clouds...
Ageing day by day...
Losing one tiny fragment at a time...
In this blinding darkness...
That gave me solace and peace...

21. The Silence Of A Martyr...

He...
He was an army man...
Who had grey hair...
With a patch of black at the back...
From the earliest memory I'd of him...
Which he said he got...
From eating fresh spinach...
Because Popeye had once said,
"I'm strong to the finich,
Cause I eat me spinach..."
He used to shave his cheeks and chin...
Every early morning...
Listening to fresh news on the radio...
With his shaving blade tracing his jaws...
In precise geometry...
And once when I went to him watching...
He had said...
The shaving blade does not hurt...
And that he could shave my invisible beard...
And I ran away smiling...
Like any little child would be...
He was strict and we were terrified...
But he kept us from harm's way...
For mom used to tell us...
When we made mischiefs...

That grandpa had a rifle still...
Despite his resignation from army...
And when we asked...
He had said...
He hid one up in the bunk...
Which he couldn't show to us right now...
Because we were kids of course...
(But trust me, he has never shown us...
I wonder if it was a lie they fabricated together...)
"He has seen too much of blood..."
I heard mom say once...
"He wouldn't be afraid...
Even when death came before him...
In reality..."
And for some part, it was true...
He refused to give up...
He refused to give in...
He was a warrior...
But didn't had the death of a warrior...
But took in the kind of death...
A common peasant faced in this century...
He was attacked by cancer...
When he passed at eighty...
And still walked around like teenager...
With the energy that could still lift a child...
In his stronger arms that had once held...
A giant rifle in war...
He refused any physical help or emotional help...
He used to say it wasn't time for his death...

No... not yet...
And he kept fighting like the warrior he once was...
Protecting his body from invasion of anxiety and depression...
Doctors loved him dear...
He was a role model for all...
A strong personality who had achieved greater heights...
And still fought through his life...
Even against death...
But it was his time... unfortunately...
And he had lost his battle...
He took a deep breath...
And gently closed his eyes...
That's what they all said...
But I couldn't believe them...
He wasn't the sort of guy...
Who would give up...
Like Dylan Thomas once said...
"Do not go gentle into that good night..."
He too mustn't have gone gently into his good night...
Instead he must've gone after fighting a war with death...
Though losing battle it was...
He's still that warrior he once was...
He died a martyr...
Leaving behind a martyr's silence...

22. Our Flag Of Defeat...

Today...
We mark the flag of defeat...
On the shining face of moon...
Because we couldn't save our home...
Our Mother Earth...
No... not yet...
Today...
We mark the flag of defeat...
On top of Mt. Everest...
Because we couldn't lift starving mass...
And give them job, shelter and food...
No... not yet...
Today...
We mark the flag of defeat...
At the bottomless seabed...
Because we couldn't save our sisters...
From domestic violence and rape...
No... not yet...
Today...
We mark the flag of defeat...
Before the Ardhanareeswara form...
Because we couldn't accept "the others..."
As humans like us with flesh and blood...
No... not yet...
Today...

We mark the flag of defeat…

Before the Yin Yang belief…

Because we forget no one is completely negative…

And couldn't see the goodness in others…

No… not yet…

Today…

We mark the flag of defeat…

Before the universal music, "Om…"

Because we couldn't accept the truth…

That God is infinite and is the ultimate truth…

No… not yet…

And finally…

Today…

We mark the flag of defeat…

Before the law…

Because we couldn't provide justice…

To the ones who actually deserve…

No… not yet…

And I wonder if this will ever change…

23. Tomorrow Morning...

Tomorrow morning...
The wind would fondle the leaves...
Announcing her departure to them...
"She won't be there..."
The wind would say...
"To direct those little streams of water...
Towards your dried up roots...
When you stand tall and proud...
When your barks dry up with age...
She won't be there anymore...
Walking beneath your proud statures...
Cleaning all the leaves you've shed..."
The ripened leaves would fall...
While the tender ones would weep...
She won't come to them anymore...
Is it their fault...?
Have they done something wrong...?
"No... no...
It isn't your fault...
But she's come of age...
And her illness robbed her life...
She's left with a smile...
But still..."
The wind wouldn't complete...
And the bark would wither...

From its vulnerable little corner...
They understood... they understood...
It's an inevitable departure...
A feeble gust of wind escapes...
From the secret chamber...
Of the leaves that are left...
Like a sigh... like a feeble sigh...
Like that unavoidable sad sigh...
Which goes unnoticed by men...
Who walk towards the house...
Both she and her husband built...
Once upon a time...
And where her five children grew up...
And after them...
Their children and even their children...
Ran around... played... and grew up...
Where footprints were left...
Carefully plucked out from memories...
I watch... sitting before her shroud...
All of them who come...
And pay respect to her...
Streams of tears and rosy faces...
I didn't knew how to cry...
To scream out to her, complaining...
Of her leaving us behind...
Asking who would eagerly wait for us now...
In that house... with foods we liked...
With our own menus...
With trembling hugs and kisses...

Her folded skin gave us...
I didn't knew...
How to scream louder...
And cry an ocean...
In front of people who came...
And tell them how much I loved her...
Or how much I would miss her...
How much hollow this house would feel...
Of how gloomy every celebration would be...
And I sit...
Sit by that river...
That has been flowing for ages...
That river...
That has seen more deaths than I've...
More departures and tears than I've felt...
And still continues to flow...
In hopes of reaching the Arabian Sea...
Like a soul's craving to merge...
With Paramaatma...
She too has become one minute drop...
Of that river now...
On a journey to reach the sea...
And I wonder...
If she'd seen us all clearly...
When she appeared in our dreams...
With a secret promise she gave me...
I await... await.. await...
For that mystery little bald baby girl...
With pink spectacles...

And a smile so wide...

My God...

I would look into her eyes and hear...

Her voice that made her promise happen...

24. #Justice_For_Me...

Some day when I'm raped...
I guess I'll be killed too...
(That's the trend now...
So that might happen...
I assume...)
Probably I'll be burnt alive...
No...
Mostly I'll be hung...
I've the correct height...
It will be easy for them...
To simply dismiss my case...
Telling my parents, brother, relatives...
And friends...
That it's a clear cut case of suicide...
And the reason could solely be...
My own fault... and mine alone...
But I've a request...
When I'm killed...
In the most brutal way...
Before my dead body...
That you would cremate later...
(If you're lucky to get my body,
Of course...
No offense...)
I want you all...

To bring out your children...
Boys and girls...
And tell them few things...
Right there...
Right then...
Right at that ages...
5... 10... 18... 22... 60...
I fucking don't care...
Just tell them few things...
Just...
Please...
Tell them...
That women are not machines...
Chaining them to houses won't help them...
(Because they'll ultimately find...
A spare key...
And then you'll be sorry...)
That what they wear isn't the reason...
That going back to home at nights...
Is at times, unavoidable emergencies...
That women already torture themselves...
Once in a month...
Further tortures can be avoided...
And... and... and...
Aaargh...
What's there to say...?
We keep saying this day in and out...
Who cares...? Who bothers...?
Probably when I die...

You'll choose my best picture...
And talk a few words about me...
Who I was for you...
And how much you loved me...
And then you end that essay long caption...
With a hashtag...
And you mourn...
And then you go back to your routine and say...
"Let's not go out at night...
Or we'll get raped too..."
Until the next hashtag...

25. I'm Sorry...

It was clouded...
My emotions...
And feelings...
And my face remained...
Just the same...
Hollow eyes with dark circles...
Sunken cheeks...
And wild ebony hair...
Sitting coldly at the table...
When he runs his eyes around...
And his words bounce off my head...
His eyes puzzled...
At the very sight of me...
Trying to decipher the meaning...
Of this indifference...
Of this frequent paralysis...
This cold numbness...
But he couldn't decipher...
Even I couldn't...
I wish I'd knew...
What made me sick...
From the very beginning...
A silent protest that died...
Some few ages before...
Crammed between the pages...

Of a book I've read recently...
A cold hatred of self...
A reclining back to my shell...
Runaway from reality...
I could spread...
Million little fragments of reasons...
But none would satisfy him...
Until he gets the exact one out of me...
And I'm unable to give the exact one out...
A severe depression of some sort...
A severe sinking back to my shell...
A severe clouding of emotions...
A lively person that I once was...
Is now as cold as a stone statue...
Left somewhere abandoned...
For ages...
With a broken nose...
And a mossy hair...
A terrible reminder of the past...
Blood oozing out now and then...
From the blinded eyes...
And deafened ears...
And lips clammed shut...
More like glued together...
Hundred dusks...
And a hundred dawns...
And a hundred more...
And another hundred...
He looks at me puzzled still...

And I look at me...
Even more puzzled...
As if trapped in some strange body...
And is desperately calling out to him...
For help...
But he seems far away...
And my sound is too silent...
But he can see something's wrong...
But not quite understand...
What's wrong...
And where it has went wrong...
And I sit silently...
With bleeding veins...
Slowly gliding into another world...
Like an abandoned ghost...
Leaving him behind...
He who loved me more...
Than anyone who actually loved me...
And understood me...
As if looking back at his own reflection...
And it was my curse...
To remain depressed...
And to be never out of it...
There was no reason to it...
No logic...
Only emotions that were clouded...
Like bottled up soda shaken wildly...
I wish I could tell him...
What bothers me...

But I couldn't tell him...

Even if I wished to...

About things I don't even know about...

Things that doesn't reflect back to me...

Things that muffle down my spirits...

Things that doesn't seem to have any form...

No logic... no reason...

No real faces...

It was my curse...

To remain uncured...

And my spirit slowly and gently glides off...

To another world...

Leaving him behind...

To mourn my funeral...

In twice the puzzle that I've given him...

When I was alive...

26. Like A Blood Red Balloon...

Like a blood red balloon...
Shaped like a distorted heart...
Filled with hydrogen...
Raises high above...
Above the darkened clouds...
My soul rise high...
And shed its rubber skin...
That bursts away when popped...
And melts into air...
Into every atom and molecule...
Into every blank space and fills...
Crammed together...
Suffocated beyond escapism...
With fragmented memories...
Of past...
Where everyone once cried for me...
"Poor little girl," they say...
"Died so young...
Hung from the ceiling...
But none saw...
Her feet hung limply...
And her lips, though, purplish blue...
And her face pale and darkened...
Still looked beautiful...

Still looked peaceful...
Her hair reflected...
The Sunday Morning Sun...
And the rays hit the window panes...
And bounced around...
Like magnets attracting magnets...
Like laser beams out of focus...
"She was great," they say...
"Once upon a time..."
None knew, none cared, none bothered...
Sudden fall from the ceiling...
Like that single raindrop...
That fall from sky...
On a summer morning...
Clearly out of season...
Clearly out of place...
And as I saw her...
Hanging just like that...
I let myself be ravished...
By all the silences that rose...
And be shrouded by darkness...
And lit with the last ray...
Of an unpleasant sunset...

27. A Writer's Secret War...

It was me who chose to write...
Knowingly how painful it might end up...
And now... the words have engulfed me...
And made me their host...
It's impossible now... for me to exist alone...
In isolation... without words and poetry...
But that choice was mine and mine alone...
And I've none to blame it upon... but me...
But the words that chose me...
It was their own choice... their own makings...
To choose me as a suitable host...
To choose to settle inside me...
And come out at often...
In every possible way they could...
It was their only choice...
And they made it long long ago...
Before I was mature enough...
To realise the intensity of that pain...
It brought me... brought me to my soul...
I've matured all through the years...
And my vocabulary has grown too...
My ideas ever changing...
As my age ascends up a steep height...
"Wow... you're a writer...
You should write...

About all sorts of serious stuff...
You should protest against this and that...
You should..."
It has made me go mad over years...
All those advises and severe misunderstandings...
Talking about misunderstandings...
Yes... I write...
I seem to have tonnes of words... and ideas...
But I've been misunderstood by many...
Many around me that whatever I said...
Never made sense to them...
And this world wasn't for me...
And will never be for me...
And I'll be pushed afar...
To a lonely cauldron...
And I'll be known as the witch...
That loiters around in dark...
"Fair is foul... and foul is fair..."
And I've to watch...
Watch everyone fade away...
My father... my mother... my brother...
My uncles and aunts...
My cousins and nephews and nieces...
And even my friends...
One by one they remove themselves from me...
One by one they cut themselves free...
"A tough child..." they would say...
And I remain afar...
In a dark room... twice removed from reality...

Scared to bits... fighting my demons alone...

Fighting my own wars... day and night...

Exhausted I sleep more...

And they all say I'm lazy...

And a useless little fellow...

But none know what it's like...

I don't claim writing is a disease...

That it gnaws me away... bit by bit...

But if I cease my words now...

Those words will take me to their world...

A world none has access to...

And I'll be lost forever...

Forever to this reality...

Where the crowd remains...

As they say...

I cannot write what I please...

Words decide what to spill...

Which part of me...

In what manner it should be...

In what font... what colour...

In what sort of paper...

The words decide...

And I'm simply a medium...

Through which they take a form...

Totally unknown to me...

And they spill out of me...

As how an ink spills from its pen...

And once I'm done...

All these words are alien to me...

As if it's not my own...
As if it'd come from some other room...
But in whatever reality it's now...
It has come from me...
And this shallow world calls me a writer...
And I smile and shrug it off...
For I've managed to spill few more words...
And had managed to survive yet another day...

28. The Mighty Fall...

A cuckoo sits perched...
On a dried up branch...
Its claws let loose...
More than few golden leaves...
That fall swirling and dancing...
To the rhythm of the autumn winds...
The bird firms its clawed grip...
And stare at the orange skies...
And bows ever so lightly...
And begin to sing...
It sings of a melodious story...
Wrapped in some melancholy of past...
Which was once much more golden...
Than those few leaves that left...
Its dried up host...
The pink skies sing along...
As the sun slowly sets...
The pink falls from the skies...
Painting the waters a deep saffron...
The cuckoo sings and sings...
Not aware of the setting sun...
The darkness slowly joins...
The poor soul's grief...
A song that springs from its beak...
Springs from somewhere deep within...

The buildings are packed tight...
And smoke rises...
Like one of those phantoms...
Melancholic in appearance...
Slowly rising to the skies...
Them too... swirling in patterns...
Curves twisted in weird angles...
But the cuckoo sings along...
Giving those phantoms a rhythm...
That erupts from its little heart...
The cold wind blows...
And the little phantoms fade...
And the leaves fall again...
The tree stands bald...
With unnaturally shaven head...
A diseased one... an old one...
And the cuckoo never stops...
The phantoms dissolve with the air...
And the leaves with the land...
And the song slowly wavers...
And find its way through...
A story hidden within...
A story that keeps flying far...
In the far distance...
Someone took its rhythm...
And kept passing it on...
The same melancholy...
That the song carried...
And the trembling cuckoo...

Never stopped...
The cold winds grew colder...
And the tree shivered terribly...
And the branch shook violently...
It was sick... the cuckoo knew...
But it never let go...
It kept singing...
Grip tightened harder...
The phantoms rose day by day...
And finally... from the jungles too...
When the orange flames caught them...
And their lungs...
They were smoked to memories...
Numerous corpses rose...
Their souls mixing up...
With those rising phantoms...
Scent of burnt flesh...
Filled the predator's nose...
With a glint in the eye...
And it was all over...
Those phantoms took the world over...
The cuckoo's song started to fade...
Over time...
As the listeners fried...
And the tree it sat on...
Gave way...
It was time for it to leave...
Its roots dug their way out...
Buried corpse...

And its shaven head hit the earth...
The rocky hard earth...
And the cuckoo flew...
Saving its last breath...
Its song ceasing to exist...
No more springs or winters to come...
No more monsoons either...
And existed only the fall...
The Mighty Fall...
And wings burned severely...
The cuckoo fell to the ground...
The last of the last...
Buried under unfathomable past...
None could read from history books...
None left to read...

29. Final Predictions...

There lived a fortune teller...
Once upon a time...
And still lives...
Who has silver eyes...
And black hair...
That curls down to her waist...
Like little serpents...
And her skin...
A rich brown hide...
Of the colour of earth...
After rain...
Petrichor...
Her perfume...
She'd a crystal ball...
And packs of tarot cards...
Spread out on her purple sheet...
She...
A mix of Bohemian and Indian...
With red, orange and yellow paint...
Smeared on her cheeks...
And golden bangles jingling...
On her slender arms...
"Lady... tell me the future...
Of this cursed land...
Tell me what is to come...

Tell me what danger awaits...

Tell me... tell me...

Tell me from your crystal ball...

Read those tarot cards for us..."

She hovered over her crystal ball...

Her palms flying over the ball...

That glows the blue of the ocean...

And her silver eyes twinkle...

With fear... with malice...?

It's very much vague...

"It's not fortune...

Definitely not fortune...

It's war that comes...

A total destruction...

The moon and the star...

Wage a war against the orange skies...

An unnatural war at hands...

The world becomes a chessboard...

And them the chess pieces...

The orange, white and the green...

At war...

When all the world's a stage...

It's not fortune, dear...

It definitely is not..."

And then she shows an image...

In thin air...

Of a total desolation...

Dry cement streets...

And burnt trees and grass...

Dust rising and dancing in the wind...
Limp leaves forced to dance...
Little cyclones rising and falling...
And rising again...
A stray dog limp around...
With its three and a half legs...
And a quarter of its tail...
Whimpering over the broken pieces...
Of her pups...
In a world that was made by Him...
For the games of beasts...
That ruled on two legs...
A little girl stutters out...
Trying to call the dying dog...
But her mother grabs her...
In her tight embrace...
And takes her inside...
Their almost crumbled house...
Where on their smudged cream wall...
Pictures fixed of Aum, Allah and Amen...
And a beaded garland...
Around the three...
Everything crumbles...
And everyone to their graves...
Graves that are to be ravished...
As dessert... later on...
And the seeds all demolished...
And traumatised...
Silence that crawls around...

Languages extinct...
And literature...
A memory of distant past...
Gods fearing those two-legged beasts...
Sit silently...
Plastered against the crumbling wall...
Ashamed of having the image...
Of those same beasts...
That resulted in this catastrophe...
The image vanished all of a sudden...
From thin air it came...
To thin air it returns...
And still... the whole world's a stage...
Shakespeare's tragedy stage...
Where everyone killed...
And everyone died...
Not even a stingy breath...
Lingers around...
"What can you do...?"
She asks abruptly...
A trace of vicious smile...
Playing at the corner of her lips...
She knows the answer...
Already...
It's evident in her smile...
Nothing could be done...
Nothing one can do about...
Something that has to be done...
By collective thoughts and minds...

I walk away more grey...
And more black and blue...
Carrying my "yet to be born child..."
In my growing womb...
My hands over them...
Trying vainly to protect...
My little cloud inside...
I was depressed...
Of my previous generation...
And my children...
Some random beasts...
With fangs and nails...
Because of my generation...
And their kids...
Simply a speck of dust...
As small as rats...
Because of their generation...

30. Goodnight Mommy...

"Dearie...
Now write about your mother...
I've seen you write...
About many other things...
But write about your mother now...
Will you...?"
I was puzzled...
Mother...?
Who the hell's a mother...?
I don't know...
I really don't...
But I try...
Wearing my black full frames...
Taking a blue feather...
I dip it in fresh black ink...
And stare at the white paper...
That lie limply before me...
I listen to the tick tock...
Of my pink watch...
It's so silent here...
Except for my pink watch...
I sit and sit and stare and stare...
But the words won't come...
The words doesn't make its appearance...
I've been blocked...

Or say...

My words have been blocked...

There's no mother...

Mother is a fictional character...

She doesn't exist...

She never did...

The tick tock grew wilder...

Louder and louder with every beat...

Of my bright pink watch...

Mata... Pita... Guru... Deva...

I've heard her chant once...

A voice...

They all called her mother...

They all did... at least...

Mother...

What's a mother...?

Who's a mother...?

I took other books...

Searched for mother...

Took a dictionary and searched...

"A woman in relation to her children..."

Could be anyone... couldn't it be...?

But still...

The meaning remained vague...

What makes her different...

From every other women...

Related to children...?

I rummaged through...

Someone who gives birth to a child...

I see... I see it clearly now...
Someone from whose womb I've born...
Mmm...
Let me think...
Oh no...
I don't remember her face...
I don't remember her touch...
I don't remember her voice...
I remember nothing...
I kick at the walls...
My foot hurts...
And I pull out my black full frames...
And stare at the wall that encloses...
I hate walls...
It scares me...
It suffocates me...
And yet...
I got no choice...
I retire...
And sink back...
Staring at the hardened wall...
Wait... what's that...?
A thick white liquid comes...
It comes near me...
It's scary...
Take it away...
Mommy... save me...
Mommy...
Is mommy a mother...?

I think so...
Take it away...
But it doesn't go...
It crawls up through a squishy pipe...
It comes to my little tummy...
I'd never seen this pipe...
I'd never seen this connecting me...
With the wall I feared...
I never...
I listen to my pink watch...
It's ticking gets slower and slower...
Something's happening...
It's growing slower...
I feel sleepy...
I feel really sleepy...
I don't think I'll wake up...
Good night mommy...
I realise what a mother is...

31. All My Sisters Started War...

I've seen them all... run away...
Escape from my evil clutches...
And my black coiling serpents...
I've seen them all...
Screaming as they ran...
A thunderstorm that has fell...
From miles above...
Splitting open the black skies...
And hitting them...
With sin smeared faces...
I've seen them all...
Pushing me aside as I went...
A pretty child...
Their curse, though...
And I felt my cheeks droop...
And my hair fall...
One by one from my scalp...
And become bald...
A witch like abomination...
And they...
They left just like that...
They all said it was me...
The witch... the seducer... the sorcerer...
Who took their souls...

Bargaining...
Handsome business...
Souls in place of black ash...
My sister Helen...
A war did start because of her...
Shurphanakha...
My other sister...
Started another war...
They claim...
All my sisters started wars...
But... but it's not true...
I've not heard of a sister...
Who began the World Wars...
It's not one of my sisters...
Who planned to liquidate Jews...
It's not one of my sisters...
Who dropped the atom bombs...
It's not one of my sisters for sure...
And indeed...
It's women who started wars...
It's women's lips that never quit...
All the worldly rumours...
It's women this...
It's women that...
But it's definitely wrong...
My sisters did no crime...
And yet we're object of blame...
Just as how I was beaten black and blue...
When my brother lost Amma's golden earrings...

32. THEY...

THEY built a wall for me...
With bright yellow and pink flowers...
Climbing all over the wall...
(I hate yellow and pink...)
And THEY made me sit inside...
Said it was better inside the wall...
Where THEY could watch me...
And I obeyed...
Sat still...
I was alright... for a while...
But then...
My brain began to grow...
Red jelly mass growing...
Pressed against dead bricks...
Growing and growing...
Until I went mad...
I pleaded...
To let me out...
But THEY never did...
I... was their pet...
And still is...
Or more like...
A wildling in a zoo...
Behind icy cold iron bars...
And moments later...

I started seeing ghosts...
Of Plath...
Of Dickinson...
Of Daddy...
Of Zhivago...
Of every single madling...
And hopeless romantics...
They kept me company...
Until it became so crowded...
And then came Achilles...
Accompanied by Patroclus...
And Circe...
And Medusa...
And Penelope and Telemachus...
And ghost of Odysseus...
And the war began...
Unnamed war...
Scarlet blood splattered...
And droplets kissed my face...
And I took a spear in hand...
And drove it right through...
Their boiling heart...
And THEY died...
And I saw with horror...
THEY died...
And THEY cursed...
"You bitch...
You'll be haunted..."
But I was already haunted...

With madness...
That THEY enclosed with me...
Within the wall...
And these ghosts...
Were nothing but figments...
Of this madness of mine...

33. Poetry From Confessions...

I sat down to write...

all the confessions of my past...

of how my life had been...

a memoir...

or an autobiography...

but never a biography...

(I trust my own words...

it's better that way...)

I sat at my desk...

my desk that faced a blunt wall...

and no views of the far afar...

of the green leaves or of a sea or river...

no winds did sing...

no birds did tune...

and I'd only a wall to look at...

and I kept looking at it...

until images were formed...

I dipped my blue feather...

in black ink...

its nib smeared in black...

I pointed it to the white paper...

and the ink fell...

a big splotch...

and I'd that splotch to look at...

for a longer while than I'd thought...

I stared and stared...
for something to come...
and the Word did come...
and I wrote it...
I kept writing and writing...
with tears welled up...
and my all-so pinky nose...
and my reddened lips and eyes...
my eyes killed me...
and my head split in two...
and when I looked at it...
it was nothing but a child's tantrums...
I crumbled those bits of papers...
like one of those pro writers...
and threw them so far away...
that they merged with my white tiles...
I lied on the desk...
with more and more white papers below...
that blotted out my tears and screams...
and I breathed heavily...
in and out... in and out...
and I wiped my tears...
tied my hair in a ponytail...
and dipped my blue feather again...
in that black ink of the night...
and I began...
once again...
until I made poetry out of it...
that poetry of my confessions...

made their way out of my heart...
and saw the light of the day...

34. Little Orphan...

I'm not sure if this is right...
I'm not sure of this gratitude...
But I'm glad that I'm an orphan...
Who sprouted out of nowhere...
In this orphanage...
I'm glad...
That my parents left me here...
Purposefully or unknown...
I'm not sure...
But I'm glad they left me here...
When they realised...
They couldn't look after me...
Any longer...
I've got many boys and girls...
Around me...
Same as me... little orphans...
I'm glad...
Their parents got rid of them too...
(No... I'm not being selfish here...
Even though you assume I'm...)
My hostel warden says...
I'm wretched...
And that's why they left me here...
But I'm glad they left me here...
I'm more glad...

That they're wise enough...
To leave us here...
I read the newspaper the other day...
And was shocked...
To see many fathers and mothers...
Accused of murdering...
Their little ones...
Fathers raping their little ones...
And selling them to his friends...
Like Barbie dolls sold in shops...
Mothers letting their boyfriends rape...
Or either smashing their little heads...
On huge rocks...
With stony hearts...
It's a terror...!!!
It's a terror...!!!
A huge terror... I must admit...
My little heart aches...
When I read all these...
My unfortunate...
Little brothers and sisters...
I'm glad my parents left me here...
I'm glad other parents did the same...
And left my sisters and brothers here...
I'm glad... I'm glad...
I'm glad they're less cruel...
And I'm more fortunate...
My sisters and brothers here...
Might not see it right...

They might think I'm selfish...
And gone nuts in my head...
But I'm grateful to God...
For giving us one more chance...
One more strike at life...
I'm glad...
That our parents left us here...

35. I'm Sick It Seems...

I'm sick... it seems...

And my sickness becomes chronic...

When exams arrive at my doorstep...

It's severe for me...

To get up from my bed...

From under the blankets...

And smile to myself and say...

"You can do it...

You're a brave soul..."

But I'm sick...

Dreadfully sick...

Depressed beyond compare...

And picking up my notes...

Are more like picking up weights...

I don't know much about maths...

But the figures on the weights...

Are more...

Than my phone digits...

And to read them aloud...

To crack the runes...

It all seems hectic...

That I lose my sense...

And I snap...

Like the strings of a kite...

And I'm thrown into the air...

And I'm poked a hole...
With a twig up above...
And caring souls ask me...
"Are you fine...?
Why were you silent...?
We're with you...
You needn't worry...
We've got your back... girl..."
But I couldn't reply...
My fingers didn't budge...
And I look at them...
And decide against...
And move on...
With my futile entertainments...
Trying to lift myself up...
Before all the sands drip down...
Like an evil tick tock...
And I slowly lift my heavy head...
And I slowly make myself get up...
And I find my senses back...
Somehow...
I manage to get up...
And read those runes...
Read them aloud...
Make sense of what I read...
Sharing my troubled sense...
With people around me...
I'm sorry...
Whose messages I've ignored...

I'm sorry...

To make you feel neglected...

But I hope you would understand...

When I say...

That I'm waging wars inside me...

A bit severe than those World Wars...

And a bit too cruel than the Nazis...

I swear...

I try to take the win-win...

And I swear...

It's an effort...

At times...

All the chicken I've eaten...

Find it hard to help me...

But I assure you...

I'm doing my best...

I'm surviving...

Even with such drastic efforts...

I do manage a win...

I do manage to be triumphant...

But...

Can you really understand...

This war that I wage...

Within myself...?

I hope you do...

I hope you do...

36. Only To Realise...

When the sun sets slowly...
You bring home a smile...
You bring home... a fake smile...
As you return from your tired work...
Tired life... tired everything...
You bring home packets...
Of sweets you made from sweat...
And pop it out of your bag...
And give them all to your kids...
And me too...
Unlike them...
I've a promise to make...
I've to listen to you about work...
And I've to hug you tight...
Under the cold waters of our rusty shower...
And you bring home...
A fake moan...
Telling me you're pleased...
But you aren't...
Because you're tired of the routine...
You want to travel...
Roam the earth...
And bring home some genuine life...
Some real smiles...
But you've got no time...

You work like an ox at field...
And you're rewarded with greying hairs...
And by the end... by the edge of your bed...
You lie down and think...
"What have I earned...
Except all these colourful notes...?"
And you're dissatisfied with the answer...
You always knew for long...
And you close your eyes...
Promising...
You'll make it right the next life...
But you fail... and fail again...
Only to realise...
You've run out of lives...

37. Sipping Coffee... And Pretending Everything's Fine...

I sit sipping coffee...

Pretending my life's normal...

But I look afar...

To the darkened skies and clouds...

And I watch them darkening further...

A thunder growls... like a mad dog...

Ready to pounce on me...

And tear me... skin to bones...

As if I've trespassed its master's lawn...

And I sip once more from my coffee...

And I pretend everything's fine...

When I look down to the streets and see...

The tar roads left deserted...

Little cardboard boxes...

Filled with people...

Rummaging through paper...

And surfing past channels after channels...

Corona spreads... and no vaccine yet...

The news keeps repeating itself...

As if a broken record's playing...

They keep looking for a change of news...

A good news to be honest...

Not the census of how many died...
And how many survived...
Now survival would be good news...
But still... they seek a different choice...
Here too... in this cardboard box too...
Strangest people keep watching series...
Movies and everything good they can find...
Pretending the world around is fine...
When only the actresses cry...
And the actors are total jerk...
Pretending half the world's still alive...
After all... Thanos did keep his word...
Half of this world survives...
Half of the people...
With their hearts broken into pieces...
Not knowing how to cope up...
The loss they've encountered...
And somewhere afar...
The war still goes on...
A silent war...
No swords clashing on armours...
Nor no bullets carving holes...
No bloodspill... no teams...
But the war still continues...
And I wonder...
If anymore Asifas or Nishas...
Or Sowmyas get raped...?
I wonder if those mentally abnormal rapists...
Are able to survive in isolation...?

Does every woman feel safe now...
With people they know...
Staying inside their cardboard box...?
Does the security cameras take shots...
Or the sirens moan into darkness...
When robbers make their way in...?
Are all the protests solved now...?
Are all the rights claimed back...?
Are people sleeping safe...
Or are they roaming around in search of food...
For their kids and beloveds...
Like stray dogs...?
Is everything fine now...?
Does every breakup feels depressive now...?
Does every heartbreaks feel light now...?
But who cares... isn't it...?
I sit by the balcony sipping coffee...
Pretending the world's fine...
Watching the first rain fall...
Remembering I've done my part...
I've grabbed those dry clothes in...
Which my mother washes every day...
In the white washing machine...
Because she wants to keep...
Her cardboard box safe...

38. Mother Earth Under Trial...

"So... you know why you're here..."
"Yes..." she replied...
Her face held the defeat...
That she knew...
Was already coming her way...
"Tell me then... Mother Earth...
Are you guilty of corona...?"
The lawyer stared at her defeated eyes...
"I'm guilty of nothing...
I'd to have revenge...
These civilised men... they raped me...
Buildings... smokes...
Tiny metal boxes with wheels...
That farted around...
And not to mention the overload..."
She cried... her sobs echoing down the hall...
Things went further around...
Colourful images started to appear...
At the back of her head...
There was a time when she was happy...
When Gods didn't have any shape...
And men didn't exist...
At least homo sapiens didn't...
And then the evolution began...

"Fuck Darwin..." she thought...

"For putting that word in her mouth...

She was promised a better life...

A responsible one...

But they went on with their axes...

And then it became the machine's job...

"Instead of tilling my fertile soils..."

She kept on thinking...

Stream of thoughts she knew...

The judge wouldn't listen...

"They went on murdering my children...

Roots and souls... all lost...

These homo sapiens...

They too were my children...

But I'm not proud anymore...

They murdered all my lovely children...

Many are long gone now...

Extinct... that's the word they use... nowadays...

Fuck them... fuck them all...

They raped me...

And called global warming... a hoax...

How could they...!!!

How could they do this to their own mother...!!!

After all... I looked after them...

And that's when I thought of Thanos...

Yes... he was a fictional villain alright...

But he had a point...

And like all those wretched mothers...

The media held villains...

I too became one...
My immunity kicked in...
And corona happened...
They're locked down...
These wretched kids of mine...
And my other kids...
They breathe now...
They're safe for a while now...
I don't know how long...
But I'm glad to see them set free...
They deserve it...
I'm glad... I'm really glad..."
She smiled crookedly...
And stared at the judge...
"No... your owner...
I'm not guilty...
I did what I thought was right...
My kids breathe peacefully now...
And I'm happy..."

39. Her Name's Samudra...

Hundred cigarette butts lie scattered...

Everywhere... in abstract art...

(Everywhere but the ashtray... of course...)

And the blood red wine...

Stains my bedsheet...

Like a woman's first blood... from her womb...

I stare in the mirror for long...

Staring at the rugged features of my face...

My square cheekbones... and my vein popped forehead...

And my Adam's apple... that remains ripe forever...

"Your dark manly face..." they say...

(With their eyes mostly...

And at times even as spittle on a hot summer noon...)

"We know you're a hijara...

You half-breed monster...

Stay away from our kids...

Stay away from us...

Your touch pollutes us..."

I watch the mascara and the foundation...

And the blood red lipstick...

Arranged neatly on the shelf...

Like files of my surgery...

And I pick myself from my bed...

The depression... pulling me down...

Stronger and harder...

And yet... I get up...
I stand straight...
My spine straight... my chin up...
I brush my teeth...
And take a shower...
And clean the ashes...
And wash the stain...
And I come...
Stand before the mirror...
Wondering what to do today...
What to do on Monday...
And what to do the rest of the day...
The rest of the week...
The rest of the month...
The rest of the year...
And I seem... at a loss...
But I know where to begin...
And as I stare at the mirror...
A memory comes clear...
Of a boy... dressing up like his deceased mother...
And his father... with his long leather belt...
Paints scarlet line on his back...
The boy ran away to a corner of his tiny room...
Crammed with books of all sorts...
Sciences... and literature...
He loved emotions the most...
He painted pictures...
Of the womanhood in him...
And wrote shocking lines...

Of the feelings that he knew best...
Tears dripped down my cheeks...
From the corners of my ocean blue eyes...
And my heart weeps a little...
Every time they shatter...
My already shattered heart...
Silent weeps... Tearless screams...
But I refuse to give up...
I refuse them... their pleasure of sadism...

40. Bloody Slut... With A Survivor Vagina...

I confess...

I watched him bleed...

I watched him bleed into the pool...

His screams muffled... his limbs tied...

He drowned...

To the bottomless fears of his...

And I simply watched him...

His helpless body...

Beat against the rushing colourless...

Like I did... mutlitple times before him...

His words came unto me...

His hands were rough against my skin...

All the time...

It's a horoscope perfect...

Us... we... like match made in heaven...

I was shy back then...

Barely twenty...

My body so thin...

It looked fragile...

I'd marks... you see...

Mostly 95/100...

But wedding was pre-planned...

His parents liked a tiny girl best...

Someone who knew cooking...

And someone obedient...
Oh... but I remember our first night...
His parents... who preferred an obedient girl...
Didn't come running to our room to save me...
From the mess I've got myself into...
Their son took things to the next level...
You see...
When Amma told she needed obedient little girl...
To be her son's little wife...
His son actually took me for granted...
And I became his sex slave...
He handcuffed me... and put me on leash...
Like a bitch... I waited by the foot of the bed...
And I still remember...
I was crying like a little girl...
Who was living in a nightmare...
I held my silence for a year...
Thought he'd change if we've kids...
And I was pregnant...
And I told him the secret...
And he slapped me across my face...
Said he hated kids...
"You're a bloody slut..."
He screamed... and lashed out...
All his anger on my back...
Scarlet lines appeared...
And I thought it was time for divorce...
I complained to my parents...
"Divorce...!!!" they screamed in shock...

"It's a shame to the family...
No one has done this in our family..."
Said my Acha...
Whom I've seen...
Painting those same scarlet lines...
On my mother's pale flesh...
When I was younger...
I felt lost...
I'd to go back to that same monster...
And let him kill my baby...
And that's when I'd the plan...
I'd to save my baby...
My unborn little one...
Was all I've got...
And I went back...
And dozed him in champagne...
And drunk he was...
Lying on the bed...
It was effort...
Dragging him to the pool...
And I tied his limbs and gagged his mouth...
Like he did to me every night...
And I stabbed him...
To his heart...
With his special carving knife...
And I pushed him into the pool...
And watched him bleed and drown...
I may be a bloody slut...
But I've a survivor vagina...

41. Plethora Of Betrayal...

Moments were blurred in a blink...
And you let loose...
All the memories we built...
Like shredded paper planes...
They danced in the wind...
And were no more...
Only veins remained...
Of the leaf you let loose from the tree...
To save me from drowning...
In my own traumatic childhood...
Did it hurt you... to walk away...
As cold hearted as a serpent...?
Did it break you... like it broke me...?
Did it mean nothing to you...
Was it all... simply fun time for you...?
Some questions went unanswered...
And you memorised my fears...
So you could poke me with them...
When I outsmarted you...
Your fangs licked my blood...
And dried me to bones...
It was just a plethora of betrayal...
That I'll never forget... ever...
Good bye... my friend...
I hope I would never see you again...

42. Just Go To Hell... If You May...

People pretend to listen...
But all they listen...
Are the shrieks of a broken woman...
And call them insane...
Locking them out of their conscience...
Like a stray bitch under rain...
I heard once...
How my friends were going crazy...
Because they couldn't step out...
And walk out of their compound...
And they look me in the eyes...
And tell me...
"I'm glad you're satisfied with books...
You mightn't be depressed... like us..."
And before I could counter that...
They turn away and walk...
And pretend I'm done with the whole topic...
Now this isn't the first time...
And this ain't gonna be the last...
I've had too much going on in my head...
I couldn't think straight...
Hanging by the pink sari...
From my white ceiling fan...
Appears an image... too real...

Sometimes... I even see myself there...

Happily dead...

Like an oxymoron I stole from my studies...

Free from this terror of the world...

They're sad... you see...

Because they couldn't travel...

And me... I'm depressed every morning...

Because I woke to my mom's call...

And I continue the day as if it's new...

But there's nothing new...

It's like every other day...

Trapped in a place that looks like home...

But it feels nothing like home...

But more like prison...

Where every dreams rot before they're born...

And it's like waiting for Godot...

You see... it's easy for Gogo...

Because he doesn't remember the previous day...

But I'm more like Didi...

With remembrance of the past...

How beautiful it used to be...

(And by past... I don't mean much of it...

I've had one of the worst past... if you may...)

But my confessions prove you nothing...

You heed to no weepings of mine...

And I'm not here at your doorstep...

To beg your mercy...

For being who I'm...

But to understand me...

As a depressed woman...
Facing her traumas... day by day...
And not as an insane...
Who needs steel chains by her ankles...
Or a banshee... who needs to be chained to trees...
But please... if you may...
Understand me before you judge...
Or just fucking keep out of my way...
And go to hell...

43. Farewell To The World Of Mortal Ignorance...

Drink my soul to the lees...
From my ripped open vein...
A swift slash... was all it needed...
And my blood splurted out...
Like a full fountain on a spring...
Filled to the brim with morning dew...
Drink my blood now...
It's fresh... find your fill...
There's plenty more to quench your thirst...
Be quick though...
Death has wore his favourite robes...
And has mounted on his favourite stallion...
Before he comes...
You've to drink my soul...
You... who led to my death...
Drink my blood and soul...
Before Death robs me from you...
Hark...!!!
Did you hear that...?
It's him... Death...
His horse's galloping hooves...
Move away now...
Take your filthy mouth from my veins...
Here comes Death...

Handsome lover of every insane minds...
His cold grey eyes fall on my pale skin...
All my blood has drained out...
It's cold... cold and dark...
And it only grows... colder and darker...
He takes me in his icy cold hands...
And his veins tickle my cold skin...
"It's cold..." I whimper...
"Hush... my dear..."
He whishpered in my left ear...
"You'll soon grow immune to it..."
And his lips moved silently towards my lips...
And he left a kiss... as cold as any ice...
I've put in my mouth when I was alive...
And he takes me with him...
It's not cold anymore...
Nor does it hurt anymore...
And no one cares about me anymore...
And I lie curled in his arms...
Looking at his eyes...
So fascinated... I could sleep forever...
Peacefully... then and there...
Not afraid of who would touch me or not...
Not afraid of who would kill me or not...
Not afraid of any nightmares that robs...
Darkened nights after nights from me...
Ah... but before I go...
I steal a glance to the mortal world...
There they cry... loudly... screaming...

Once... when I was alive...
They used to tell me...
Suicidal thoughts were fun...
And depression was a hoax...
Oh... now they weep...
Weep like someone dear to them had died...
You don't think it's funny anymore... do you...?
You don't think it's a hoax... do you...?
You'll punish yourself... until you die...
For your ignorance...
Let me slip...
From your fragile palms...

44. Confessions Of A Prostitute...

There was a time when I was younger...
When I'd a father and a mother...
Not the ones like yours though...
But the sort of namesakes...
My father loved men...
And my mother was a drug addict...
Both of them needed money...
So I'd to teach myself all the alphabets...
The little kids nearby helped me learn...
And gave me their left over crayons...
And paper... to sketch...
And all was good until one day...
My father took me out for a walk...
I remember that day...
I just turned sixteen...
And for the first time...
My parents bought me a cake...
"Where are we going daddy...?"
I remember asking...
And he smiled smoking his cigarette...
The fumes dissolved...
Into the darkened night...
And his teeth were all yellow...
And his lips were all black...

"It's all gonna be fine, my plum...
You'll be as good as new..."
He mumbled through the smoke...
And I watched the path disrupted...
And a little of it made its way...
Into my ocean blue eyes...
My mother was all knocked out...
Drunk and wasted off...
Back in our little house...
"Mommy's alone..."
I remember saying...
"None of it matters little one..."
He assured me...
And we went into this huge house...
I remember...
Looking around the architecture...
The beautiful pillars...
The smooth floors...
And the unimaginable ceilings...
A man came laughing...
From one corner of the huge house...
"Is that Santa...?"
I asked stupidly...
And oh...
I remember he laughed at me...
He said I was funny...
And gave me cakes...
And juice...
And I had it all...

When my father said I could...
We three talked for a while...
And I liked him very much...
"How about we see the playroom...?"
He asked me with a smile...
And my father nodded at me smiling...
Lighting yet another cigarette...
Which he pulled out magically...
From his coat pocket...
I went with him to the playroom...
And oh... it was such a beautiful one...
There were huge teddy bears...
And very pretty dolls...
And beautiful dresses...
And tea party set...
"They belong to my daughter..."
He said smiling...
And I nodded and walked towards them...
And that's when I heard a click behind me...
I don't need the brains...
Of a twenty year old to understand...
What was to happen...
He took of his shirt...
And his pants...
And a strange thing...
Hung from between his legs...
It made me sick...
I wanted to run away...
But I was paralysed...

And the door was blocked...
By this huge Santa...
He grabbed my tiny body in his huge hands...
And pushed me hard against the floor...
The floor was so cold on my back...
Oh... how clearly I remember it all...
"Daddy..." I cried...
"Daddy... help me... Daddy..."
But he didn't climb up the stairs...
I thought he killed him...
And the horror paralysed me further...
And made it all easy for him...
I closed my eyes...
Tears rolling down my cheeks...
I kept my eyes shut tightly...
And bit my lips...
Every time he pushed inside me...
And when all was over...
He threw a fresh pink dress for me...
One that belonged to his daughter...
(He tore mine... I couldn't wear them...)
And he held my hand...
And we walked down...
I could feel the blood dripping down...
My little legs...
Felt more weaker than before...
And I saw my father...
Smiling at me...
Lighting another cigarette...

Which he pulled out from his pocket...
"How's my little plum...?
All good to go...?"
He asked with a wider smile...
As the fat Santa...
Placed colourful papers in his palm...
Father took me everywhere...
Every night...
He was rude to me when I'd my periods...
And adviced me...
Never to get pregnant...
But one day...
I ran away...
With a little bit of his money...
And survived on it for a week...
But what job...
Could an uneducated girl get...?
And so I'd to visit men after men...
Again...
But one night... it all ended...
The news headlines kept talking about...
An unidentifiable rotting corpse...
Under a bridge...
Whose skull had a hole...
No family took me away...
No ritual cremation was done for me...
Instead they simply threw me in fire...
And closed the case...
I wonder...

Where my father and mother was...
I wonder...
If they're still alive...

45. "Hey Bro... Chill..."

"Hey Bro... Chill...

Why are you angry all the time...?

What the hell is wrong with you...?"

If someone where to ask this...

I would stay silent...

And pretend you're an asshole...

Because in reality... you must be...

Or else you wouldn't ask this question...

Every ten in a twenty child get sexually abused...

Leaving trauma behind as a scar...

That fills his or her life with fear till eternity...

Yes... Boys get sexually abused...

Even raped...

You don't know...?

How ignorant can you be...?

Every woman who chooses her path...

Who chooses her style of dressing...

Her lifestyle of being single...

Or her opinion not to have kids...

Will be labelled as sluts...

Or in Malayalam... *Vedi*...

Marriage is a life-changing divine event...

But because woman's choices aren't meant...

They run away frightened of their day...

Where they can shine like a diamond...

But hoping that such a day would come delayed...

Why am I pessimist... You ask...

Lemme tell you then...

I've not known peace in my life...

Because wherever I go...

I'm forced to get panic...

Look around in 360 degree...

Whether someone's following me or not...

You ask... Why I'm worried about things...

That does not affect me...

But unfortunately... It does affect me...

And is a concern for my kids... Some day...

And for their kids...

It's a concern for every sister I know...

It's a concern for every mothers... Aunts...

And whatnot...

I used to believe that clothes were the issue...

Until I learned that a lady in burqa...

Got raped...

I thought the problem was in our curves...

Until I learned that a baby in a diaper...

Got raped...

I thought the problem was because...

A girl walked around at night...

Partying with her boyfriend...

Until I realised a wife who was with her husband...

Got raped... Right infront of him...

I thought a pregnant woman would be spared...

Until I learned that a pregnant woman...

Got raped and hung on ceiling...

When nobody was around...

And I thought...

That a woman infected with Corona...

Would be spared...

For fear of infection...

Until I learned she was raped in an ambulance...

What more should I learn...?

Being a daughter of India...?

What should I teach my kids...?

That it's not safe to step out...

Without a pepper spray...

Or at least a black belt in karate...?

Or should I teach them to smuggle a gun...

With six bullets...

And a pendant of cyanide...

If worst comes to worst...?

And bro...

Don't fucking call me bro... or bruh... or whatever...

Call me my name...

Everyone has their name...

And so do I...

46. Revised Indian Pledge...

India is my country...
All Indians are my brothers and sisters...
(Except few brothers can rape few sisters...
Just so they're born sisters...
With fully functional vaginas...)
I love my country...
And I'm proud of its...
Rich and varied heritage...
I shall always strive to be worthy of it...
(But it seems that high caste boys...
Can cut off Dalit tongues...
If they begin to sing...
Proudly of their Bharat Mata...
Because India has become the land...
Solely for high castes...
And rich...
And the low castes and poor...
Are not worthy of this country...)
I shall give my parents, teachers and all elders...
Respect and treat everyone...
With courtesy...
(Even if our father rapes us...
Even if our mother lets her boyfriend rape us...
Even if our guru sticks his lust...
Inside our mouths that knew only...

A, B, C, Ds...
Even if our uncle likes to put his hands...
Inside our skirts and trousers...
Respect is a must...
And we'll respect all our elders...
And history that talks of Babri's fall...
Not withstanding wind...
Because even our law can't withstand this wind...
How could anyone expect Babri to withstand...?)
To my country and my people...
I pledge my devotion...
In their well-being and prosperity alone...
Lies my happiness...
(Even when a huge number of kids like us...
Kill ourselves daily...
Because we're afraid of our cut off tongues...
And broken ribs...
And bleeding holes...)
Bharat Mata ki jai...

47. I'm Angry Tonight...

I'm angry tonight...
I'M ANGRY TONIGHT...
I'M VERY VERY ANGRY TONIGHT...
Does this make you afraid...?
No... It doesn't...
Because that's what movies have taught you...
Angry women... are either cute or hysterical...
Or even a ghost...
I belong to none...
But I'm angry tonight...
And I'm severely hopeless tonight...
The sun that comes out tomorrow...
Does not hold happiness for me...
Nor for any woman in India...
The moment the sun rises...
The thought of a predator lurking around...
Frightens us...
Then... not to mention the nights...
I'm angry tonight...
Because I'm India's daughter...
And for that very reason...
India decides to chop off my tongue...
I deserve the right to speak...
Scream even...
But no...

You'll arrive at our footsteps...

Charge me with treason...

For speaking ill of India...

And her leaders...

And you'll chop off my tongues...

And whatnot...

I don't know...

But you won't do anything to me...

Until you rape me...

Because a girl whose tongue chopped off...

Is ugly to you...

I'm angry tonight...

Because you promised to bring peace...

And yet you disrupt the country...

You bring chaos...

And you rescue the culprits...

Hey you... who consider you love your God...

More than us...

Let's just say... God's not happy with you...

Not happy...

But angry... Very very angry...

So angry that the god you worship...

Is boiling like volcanic lava...

Ready to erupt...

And turn you to ashes...

Hey you... you...

My god... I can't speak...

I'm so angry tonight...

Because I'm ashamed of my childhood...

When I used to pledge...
"India is my country..."
Every morning...
Because India is definitely not country...
India is my death knell...

48. Getting Even...

You left a broken twig...

Hidden in my shoes...

And I left a frog trapped in yours...

I thought we were even...

But then the frog leapt up...

Landed on your face... and peed...

I swear I feel guilty...

For being the one who laughed the most...

I do...

You left a scorpion sting in mine later on...

And now... I lie motionless... shrouded...

I guess we're even now...

And I don't know why you weep...

Before my white cotton shroud...

But the incense sticks smell so great...

I wish you'd found the scorpion in your first try...

49. Timed Out Mother...

She sits by the fire...
Rocking on her favourite chair...
Smile hanging on by the corner of her lips...
Humming a song she'd heard from her mother...
Her fingers busily knitting a sweater...
Not pink... Not blue...
But lavender...
Which she believed had both...
She rocked back and forth...
As the clock struck midnight...
When the sweater was finally done...
She walked to the little grave by the house...
Where her husband had buried their little one...
Like poisoned calf whom he buried a week before...
She laid out the sweater on the grave...
And smiled at her baby...
But her baby was already frozen in the depths...
Her warmth seemed far-fetched...
And timed out...
Just like the smile that had faded from her lips...
The day her baby died...

50. Cry For Help...

Does it have to be like this...
This hard to hold onto what we fell in love with...?
Does it make sense when you do what you do...
And I don't do what you do...
Do you miss me when you're away...
When you prevent yourself from texting...
When you prevent yourself from calling...?
Does it hurt... my absence...
Does it make any sense to you...?
Or is it just me... hanging on by the last string...?
Oh please... please tell me I'm not the only one...
Tell me I'm not alone in this journey...
But I don't think I understand it...
I feel invisible... like a failed science experiment...
My depression is all I can blame... for now...
Until I reach a new conclusion...
A new reason to blame...
But my depression at its fault...
It gets darker now...
The dark clouds are heavier now...
And it drowns me in a stenchy pool...
Of further darkness...
I'm sorry... I'm sorry you cannot help me...
It's not your fault... not your lack...
I do want to explain how it works...

Because I clearly know how it does...
But I've got no words...
I've got nothing...
I keep drowning still...
And oh... you're far away on the shore...
Miles and miles above the sea level...
And you look into my eyes...
And ask what's wrong...
But I'm nowhere near you...
Those longitudes and latitudes...
Does not work under this dark sea...
I'm sorry for your loss...
And I'm sorry I worsened it...
Out of all people you've met...
You shouldn't have met me...
Maybe then I could've left this drowning...
Without a look back... over my shoulder...
And you... you could've lived happier still...
As if nothing had ever happened to you...

51. Midnight Conspiracy...

You ask me... no... you order me to sleep early...
And wake up early... like most people do...
But unfortunately... I'm not most people...
I'm different from most people...
You tell me that my writing is just a phase...
That I'll stop writing once I'm married...
Damn you... if that's true...
I'll hate my husband and children...
Who'll be responsible for my ceased writings...
For the rest of my life...
Because I know it's not a phase for me...
It's redemption...
You order me to listen to meditation music...
Right before I close my eyes...
You advice that I'll sleep better...
But tell me what I should do...
When words cloud my senses...
And whimper like a sick baby at midnight...
Begging me to take a pen and paper and write...
Tell me which meditating songs are powerful enough...
To stop my words and my building up sentences...
Tell me what I should do to break down...
Every deep structure that comes disguised as a surface structure...
When you snore by my side...
Not knowing the troubles my brain goes through...

You order that me being an introvert is the issue...
That if I began talking...
Maybe my writing will cease...
And I'll be normal...
But you're not true...
Because you know what...?
Me being an introvert does not mean I'm shy...
It only means there's no one out there...
Who shares an interest in my existential crisis...
And conspiracy questions...
You look from under the comfy covers you've tucked yourself in...
But even you cannot tell me why I exist where I exist...
Then how do you think I would ever be interested to talk to you...?
Tell me why you think that I should stop writing...?
Because my darling...
From the point I stand...
You're way stupid than the people I've met so far...

52. Hollowed Happiness...

I feel hollow...

How empty can happiness make one feel...!

I've turned myself into that greedy man...

Who received a boon once...

That all his tears would turn into pearls...

I've got this boon...

That all my years would turn into depth...

Unfathomable depth that even Pacific couldn't handle...

And in my depth lurks monsters and aliens...

That even I myself haven't discovered yet...

Don't get me wrong...

I don't want unhappiness struck upon my shoulders...

But yes... I do miss the depth that I'd...

And those strange monsters who lurked beneath...

Haunting my life from behind the veil of darkness...

Can a person make someone happy...

As happy as this...

As happy... as if the person loses their depth...?

Like a curious child... I've too many questions...

But I'm not sure... if you have answers to all those...

Maybe you're shallow... or maybe happiness made you shallow...

But whatever it may be...

I've lost my depth...

And the ocean that I once was...

Has turned dry...

And I bet... Atlantis was inside me...

Because in that dryness... I see an island rising...

And it looks like... Atlantis has popped up...

Is this my end... my end as a writer...?

I'm afraid... I'm too afraid to think...

I hope not... cause I want to taste words once again...

Much better than I taste them now...

53. Tagore's Tears...

Walking through a lonely street...
On an Indian summer midday...
By the far end... round the corner...
A shadow lurked beneath...
What was once... a great banyan tree...
Chanting India's National Anthem...
Over and over again... in a monotonously drained voice...
As if trying to edit those lines...
That once gave us all goosebumps...
Walking closer to the shadow...
I saw... his cotton white beard...
And his eyes... glistening like diamonds...
Alas... he was crying silently...
His face seemed oddly familiar...
At which I looked for what seemed like hours...
His face resembled to those pictures I've seen...
By the corner of India's pride... *Gitanjali*...
The shadow... after moving around restlessly...
Sat down... whimpering soundly like a little child...
As if someone had denied his lolly pop...
Tagore... whom we all came to respect...
Whom we all took to our hearts as our pride...
Now whimpers like a child...
His face buried in the dry dusty Indian floor...
Is it safe...

My thoughts kept troubling me...
To ask a phantom why he's crying...?
Or is it someone in Tagore's clothes...
To lure women to his abode...?
I waited for a while... and for another while... and an another...
Until his whimpering grew strong...
And I'd no choice but to ask him...
But oh... I made sure I was farther from him...
If it were a prank...
(Cause you know... India is unsafe for women...
And every law is in favour of rapists and molesters...
We women are Ashuddh... we women are sluts...
Men... no matter whatever crap they do...
Are the heroes of their Mother India...)
"It's me child... I'm Tagore..."
He whispered as if he read my mind...
"But I'm not proud anymore... of my India...
I'm not proud... all I feel is disgust..."
He kept chanting illegibly...
For what felt like another hour...
It was so silent... even during a midday...
That I could hear my watch ticking...
And my heart beating louder...
I'm not supposed to talk to strangers...
Let alone men...
Is it okay if he's a phantom...?
I'm not sure... did the court say anything about talking to a phantom...?
He kept crying... and I stared at him with a face that apologised...

He knows... I guess... he knows...
What else could destroy his pride...!
I kept a watch on him... that was all I could do...
Until he was done with his tears...
But oh no... it seemed much more than Ganga's waters...
And much more saltier than the Pacific...
My mouth felt parched...
Not by the Indian sun... but by the Indian laws...
I silently bowed my head with shame...
And turned around and walked back home...
In the far distance... I could feel...
Tagore's tears fading...
His phantom shrinking...
I wonder what the rest of our ancestors feel...?
Do they feel that same embarrassment...?
I don't know... I may never know...

54. Censor Me If You Can...

Write about nature...
Write about love...
Write about positive stuff...
Write about parents...
Write about relatives, teachers and friends...
Write about the sunlight...
And not the witch who flies at night on her broomstick...
Nor the werewolf who come out at full moon nights...
Write about mothers who serve...
Not about mothers who suffer from post partum depression...
Write about that boyfriend who earns money for you...
Not about the girlfriend who tries to get a job to support him...
Write about that wife who's illicit relationship...
Not about that wife whose face and ribs are broken...
Write about goodness... be optimistic they say...
When the world clearly speaks differently...
Write poems with beautiful words...
Censor on those that use words like "fuck"...
I'm tired of these advices...
Which has become my daily routine...
I'm frustrated, angry and annoyed...
Of how they teach us to ignore...
What should be addressed in the first place...
About teachers who tell that girls are reason for their rapes...
Tell me what reason a 9 month old baby gave...

We live in this world...

Where somebody once said that a 9 month old was asking for it...

When she lifted her legs and smiled at the abuser...

What the fu... No...

I'm not allowed to use that word...

I'm censored...

I'll be silenced by beeps if I were to say all those...

These themes have become a cliché...

Too much we've discussed...

Too much we've suppressed...

I'm done...

I'm fucking done...

We are fucking done...

Censor me if you can...

But I ain't gonna stop...

55. Anxieties On Marrying A Stranger...

Our ancestors... they'd no anxieties...
In getting married to a stranger... they'd say...
Because they never had a lover...
They were decent women...
But youngsters... they're immoral...
Finding an excuse to marry their loved ones...
Our ancestors... they'd no anxieties...
As they stepped onto the *mandap*...
With a stranger... who wore white shirt and white dhoti...
His moustache spiked up with oil...
That he himself squeezed out from a coconut...
(No hard feelings dear... I'm strong enough to protect you...)
Our ancestors... they'd no anxieties...
As they stepped into their room with a stranger...
Whose eyes hungrily roam around their body...
With a secret packet tucked beneath their pillow...
(Not all men... not all men dear...)
As they talked about their dreams to fulfil...
They only looked at your lips...
Having fantasies of ripping them apart...
Our ancestors... they'd no anxieties...
As they got beaten up like dough for chappati...
"Add a little ketchup will ya...!"
They add... a little spice to top it up with...

But oh no... I'm scared... I've anxieties...

I'm worried of my husband beating my teeth out of my mouth...

I'm afraid of the person... breaking my ribs...

Just because he didn't like them...

When they poked against his chest... as we made love...

I'm afraid of a man... who comes sneaking into my room...

And forces me into his game... and leave me soaked in my sweat... and tears...

"Hush...!" My ancestors voice their fear...

"Young girls aren't allowed to talk of that...

You girls should dream... but not too much...

You're to serve your husbands...

Like you serve God..."

All of these takes my breath away...

What should I do... I'm not sure...

If I were to protest to this...

Will I've to force myself into atheism...?

I do not know...

56. I Watch You Go...

Your tongue kept swirling around those insults...
You threw at me daily...
Those silent whispers that left by the opened window...
Like the sighs rising from a dying child...
Holding onto her last breath...
I too held onto you... like a leech...
Sucking off what's left of your love... that I could get...
But you were anemic for me...
Dried off from every angle...
You told me... you could love me better than I could...
And I trusted you... even though I sounded selfish in my head...
But then... it was time for your connotations to fall into place...
That underlying meaning sticking onto the walls of the sieve...
Like they were reluctant to pass through...
And I saw that dirt in them... that ugly black powdery words...
Whenever you told me you loved me... more than I do...
I kept seeing that black powder grains...
Silently making their way to the walls of the sieve...
Sticking onto it...
Like a baby sticking onto its mother's womb...
And silently... very silently...
I watched you go... walking away to the horizon...
Where I could never meet you...
And I don't want to...
Because it's over... it's never the same again...

And all of a sudden... you realise it's goodbye time...

And you tell me you loved me always...

But unfortunately... I could never feel... for your love was like an electric current... and I was a mere rubber...

• 145 •

57. When Demons Of My Past Pilot My Brains...

My body aches nowadays...

Especially my shoulders...

Especially my head...

Especially my back...

Especially everywhere...

My body aches in such a manner...

That it reminds me of the pilots of my body... some dark demons of past...

They've used my body mercilessly...

Like a pilot... who hates his airplane...

And suddenly... my body began to break apart...

With creaking noises... with every single move...

My body aches nowadays...

With rust smelling from all pores of my skin...

The disgust it brings... in other people's eyes...

It seems... I've begun to rot much before my death...

And my death... is only a secondary concept on its way...

I can hear... right above my shoulder...

Those silent deep breaths of death...

And moments like these...

I would wish if I actually died...

But that's the torture...

I'm cursed to be trapped inside a rotting fleshy house...

And two-storeyed haunting house...

With antiques from India, Egypt and Persia...

And slowly... every artwork I've hung begins to fall...

With their rough steering of my brains...

Those demons of my past...

They find their way through the food I eat...

Through the little drops of water I drink...

And even through those invisible oxygen molecules...

That find their way through my damaged nostrils...

I'm tired... I'm exhausted...

I don't think there's any better way to tell you this...

But... I'm exhausted...

Kill me if you want... I beg you...

But don't let me live like this...

My body has become a junk...

And my soul has already been tamed by the devil...

It's over... I feel those silver chains burning my flesh...

I smell that roasted flesh...

Filthy... filthy with demons of my past...

Leave me... leave me the fuck alone...

58. Wishes Of An Eleven Year Old...

It was a Sunday evening...

When suddenly... there was a huge crowd outside...

Amma should've come home last night...

But she was running late...

Said she was busy... said she'd make it up to me... and I trusted her...

Today... I woke up early...

Hoping she'd come early with my favorite chocolates...

But no... no one came...

I waited and waited... until grandma asked to sleep a little while more...

I waited in my room... pretending to be asleep...

(I couldn't sleep... you know...)

It was horrific... why was Amma late...?

She never goes silent as this...

It was almost seven... when I watched the darkening skies...

Lit with red and blue lights... with sirens that I could swear... I never wanted to hear ever...

But the lights came nearer until the white shrouded van spit out my white shrouded Amma...

She was a nurse... an angel... others would call her...

I know how she died... I heard her go out of breath through the phone once...

They made me wear plastic covers...

(I thought plastic was banned...)

And they gave me more plastic to cover...

One man...

(I've seen him before...)

He told me that Amma had died a warrior...

That she fought bravely... until her last breath...

I silently stood and listened...

What more comments could a shocked eleven year old could give...!

I nodded... and watched as they silently burnt my Amma...

The flames rose to the dark skies...

And I hoped Amma would rise like a phoenix...

But no... she was no angel... nor was she a phoenix...

If the gods Amma had trusted did save her...

She would've been alive...

At night... I couldn't sleep... nor could I cry...

I thought about my friend whom Amma cured back to life...

He'll be happy now... he can go see more *poorams* in future...

But I'll never see her again... at least not in this life...

59. Scrambled Eggs/Brains...?

I think my brain looks like scrambled eggs...
I can hear that hissing sound at times... that they make on hot frying pan...
And at times... I can smell... that fried smell without salt...
I guess my blood has more carbon dioxide...
Like a bubbling up Coca-Cola bottle...
Who gobbled up 100 packets of Mentos...
In its Coca-Cola filled belly...
I think this is what online classes do to us...
"You don't have to come to class..." says the teachers...
"Do this... do that..." they say...
"You don't have to go to classes..." says parents...
"Do this... do that..." they say too...
And I think I'm stuck...
Not able to breathe...
Not able to stay afloat...
You see... that's what I go through...
And I guess... that's what you go through too...

60. Afraid Of Losing My Words...

Ages ago... I used to write...

When words bled out through my veins...

Like it was nothing... a piece of cake one might say...

And I used to believe that I would continue writing...

Forever and ever...

But I'm scared right now...

Scared that they would abandon me...

Like I abandon people...

For fear that I'll hurt them...

Yes... I've my trust issues tucked in deeper...

Like a little child tucked inside a blanket...

Waiting for a bedtime story...

Pretending to fall back asleep...

Only to wake up in the middle of the night...

Demanding one more story...

But I'm scared...

Scared my words would abandon me...

But I've got no excuses...

No space to cry out loud...

They say they understand me...

But most of them...

They don't hear those silent screams...

Escaping like demented soul...

From a body dead and rotten...

I guess... this is what they do... my demons...

They steal everything from me...

Everything that I trust...

Everything I love...

And this eats me alive...

Wait... wait a second...

How did I start...

This poem...

Oh yes...

How I fear my words would abandon me...

Cause then I'll be really lonely...

61. Let's Light A Candle...

I cannot hide my fear any longer...
The world... it has turned into its worst...
You ask... in this light of day...
Why we all need feminism...
As you joke about it...
As you drink your dry scotch...
In the middle of the night...
Howling and screaming with your friends...
Guarding your bro-codes with your lives...
While your free hand...
Tightens its grip around the necks...
Of the women of your life...
As your loud laughter...
Spits stains on their lives...
That once had dreams... once had hopes...
You see... the numbers aren't falling down...
The names aren't forgotten...
Of all those lovely women...
Who once dreamt of being somebody...
Somebody who brought a change to this world...
But all you did was laugh at her...
Told her that her dreams were nothing...
That she deserves no dreams...
And you held her down...
With your boots on her neck...

How many... how many more...?
How many candles should I light...?
How many *deepas* should I light...?
How many bathes in Ganges will let me save my soul...
From these cursed lands...?
How many... how much...!
I' m tired of screaming...
This darkness... and this silence grows...
And somewhere in this darkness...
I can smell... the scent of melting candles...
You've failed... you civilised... you evolved... species...
You've failed in your evolutions...
I guess... if there's a God at all...
The God will be disappointed...
That God will be so disappointed...
They've not even slightest of hopes...
On a better future...
You've failed...
I repeat...
You civilised...
You evolved...
Good for nothing species...
You've failed...
And in the far end...
Burns a million more candles...
And a million more names carved...
On the crumbling stone wall...
Screaming back at the living...
You've failed...

62. It's Time To Say Goodbye...

I guess... you've become nothing but a fog now...
Silently present...
Visibly confused...
And completely distant...
You've become one of the ghosts from the past...
Your face glitching... like a faulty display...
Showing faces of all those ghosts from the past...
You loiter around this veranda...
Where you've played before...
Where your jokes have echoed...
Where your silences lingered...
Did it hurt you when they burnt you...
When your bones turned to ashes...
When your silences became eternal...?
Did it make any sense when all those darknesses...
Turned into endless fog...
Stretching out into endless paths...?
I'm not afraid of you... your ghost...
But I can see you...
Looking from behind locked doors...
Smiling to justify me...
That your decision seemed right to you...
And only to you...
Do I miss you...?

I don't know...
Should I miss you...?
I don't know that either...
I guess... I'm still confused...
My brain refuse to register certain details...
My brain... it keeps finding excuses...
It keeps asking questions...
It keeps denying truths...
That's right there... right in front...
I don't know...
My answers have not found its way out...
Maybe... it's for the best...
Maybe it's for your best too...
I don't know...
You should go now...
You should fade into distance now...
You can no longer linger behind...
I might see you...
But I hope not...

63. I Think I'm Tired...

I think I'm tired...
Of all the comparisons that revolve...
Around my aching head...
The marksheet displayed in bleeding red...
Right infront of my eyes...
When the whole world has become competitive...
I... struggling to survive...
Every single day...
I think I'm tired...
My heart aching...
To find some meaning in this world...
To find some connection...
That brings a meaning to my life...
Every meaning leading to yet another...
And I... silently wishing if all were okay...
That my worries were nonsense...
But the pain is real... very real...
And it breaks my heart...
That I'm too sensitive...
And I would give anything...
To take it back...
But no... I've already sold my soul to Muse...
My words demand my ache...
And I'm tired... God... I'm tired...
I would love to sleep just once...

Not fearing... not soaking my pillow in tears...

Not making my life all about my anxiety... and anti-depressant pills...

I'm tired... I know I'm tired...

The food I eat tastes of metals...

And the sleepless nights are lonely still...

Oh God... can I come to your abode...

And sleep without a drop of fear...?

Can I please... end this life...

And begin a new one...

As merely a lifeless particle...?

I'm tired... I know I'm tired...

My eyes give you all the proof you need...

I'm tired... I know I'm tired...

64. The Fading Shadow...

The corridors went silent...
The noises almost fading...
As the winds blew the leaves around...
And the trees bowed gently to the silence...
There appeared a shadow...
In the far corner...
Almost went unnoticed...
Almost ignored by the bustling leaves...
The shadow stood silent...
As the last person walked around the corridor...
The keys dangling at her finger tips...
As if she were a fabled gate keeper...
The shadow watched... silently... brooding...
It could smell the scent of despair...
Somewhere looming around the corridors...
The shadow watched... and watched... and watched...
And finally... somebody saw the phantom shadow...
And it looked... just looked...
No comments... no movements...
But just... watching the silence that haunted those corridors...
The shadow licked its lips...
The silence tempting...
The despair... hanging down its throat...
Like a medal... its victory silently lurking around the silence...
And then as it watched...

The voices of memories past...
Echoed in the hallway...
Voices of happiness...
Voices of hope...
The shadow frowned...
Its face shrivelled at the very thought of happiness...
But the voices echoed...
Voices that kept flowing down the cracked up walls...
Voices that kept rushing down the hollow windows and doors...
And then the shadow thought...
Thought harder of whom the voices belonged to...
Cringed at the very thought of how they made...
Evolved this dull looking building...
How they painted a rainbow in nothingness...
With nothing more than their laughter...
And the shadow... vanished into nothingness...
The silence vanishing with it...
And once again... the voices kept flowing...
Flowing like it would never end...

65. Post Partum...

My baby monster screams...
Her voice... an alarm ringing inside my brain...
Waking me up from a sleep I barely had...
Last night... it ached... right there...
From where she shot out from my body...
The brutal stitches done neat...
And the night seemed darker than usual...
My baby monster screams...
Her sound echoing... and echoing...
Even after she's slept...
Even after everyone has slept...
Even after the whole night has slept...
My baby monster screams...
Day and night... and night and day...
Her teeth not popped out...
Her fat devilish body...
Brutally torturing me...
My baby monster screams...
Even when I'm done with her...
Even when someone else has taken her...
Even when they praise her...
Her little round face...
All messy because I never fed her...
They say... they say...
It's all my fault... that milk won't come...

They say... they say...
I'm a bitch of a mother...
My baby monster screamed...
And she won't... she won't again...
Ah...! The relief... the silence...
I put my fat baby monster in a bag...
And left her on the shores of the river...
Her fat body reeking of death...
Her fat body eaten by maggots...
And they say... they say...
I've killed my baby daughter...
For I don't recall doing any of it...
My baby monster screamed...
Though... she'll never again...

66. Im'mortal...

The embalmed darkness envelopes me...
The noises of shrieking women drives me mad...
Both are faded as they reach me...
The scent of my blood under my skull reeks louder...
I crave to muffle my ears...
With my hands that lie dead beside my body...
Chained in invisible grey threads...
Of this bitter-sweet truth that seized me so soon...
The shrieks grow louder around me...
But my ears focus to the gentle whispers around...
Of priest that guides my little relatives...
Towards the rituals that give me peace as I ascend to the skies...
My eyes are closed as I listen to them in peace...
The voice resonate as I count the seconds into minutes...
Into hours that I'd be left with a body...
That I've grown too fond of in this world of mine...
No, no... the world isn't mine...
It must've been mine when I was alive...
Not now, not really, the world belongs to the ones alive...
Skies are the abodes of the ones that are dead...
I count and count in my head...
It seems frightening to leave this place...
That has grown so familiar over time...
And suddenly did the wailing become loud...
Everyone seemed eager to know...

Why I was dead so early...
The news spread all over the cosmos...
That I killed myself out of a fear...
Was I pregnant with an infant...
Of a devil that has done me wrong...
Or had I had a lover guy...
Who raped me of my purity...?
Should I wake and slap them across...
Or should I grab their hands and pull them to my pyre...
Or should I wake as a Banshee at nights...
And haunt their conscious to death...?
As I plan my revenge hands wrapped me in white cloth...
Wrapped me whole muffling my nose and mouth...
Why didn't they let me breathe...
Don't they know they suffocate me...?
I looked around, one last look...
Before they suffocate me and accept my downfall...
Has he come to see me...
Has he brought a wreath with flowers that I despised...?
Yes, I'd a handsome lover...
Someone who cared... not who raped...
Someone who loved me more...
More than his own dear life...
And yet I gave up, I was no fighter...
I let my breath escape one last time...
He was there in a corner with reddened eyes...
Imagining that I was breathing still...
It was a final goodbye... I've left forever...
Shut my eyes tighter and rigid...

For I couldn't watch him whimper...
Like a little baby in a masculine body...
What was so permanent about the body...
What's so special about it...
I've left mine to be burnt to ashes...
The body everyone said were too lean and ugly...
I was carried so close to that lonely tree...
On one side of my humble house...
That has turned to a hell as time passed...
And my heart could bear no more...
I was gently kept down...
With firewood neatly placed above...
Someone gave the fire...
That engulfed my fragile body...
I'd bones, nerves, brain and heart...
I was made just as everybody else with flesh and blood...
I'd feelings that ruled my conscious...
I'd tears that weren't shed when I was alive...

67. Letter From Dead Wives Of Tomorrow...

I feel like one of those dead wives...

The only difference... is that I haven't married yet...

And when I scream that I'm afraid...

Afraid of a lot many things...

People say... it's fine... it's better than the last... it's better than the next...

And I scream back...

I don't want a last... nor a next...

Let me be... let me be...

Let me do what I'm good at...

Let me paint... let me write...

Let me read... and let me learn...

Let me go over a line...

And let me learn a new skill...

(Is it too hard to learn a ukulele...

Or is it ok if I stick to keyboard...?)

And I want to learn how to take photographs...

Edit them... and make the world see through them...

The world... the angles... the nooks and corners...

That they've never seen before...

And let me... let me put a hibiscus on my hair...

And call myself mad...

Mad with hunger of the art...

And the words that I can taste...

And let me... let me please...

I beg you...

Let me please have a room of my own...

Where I can be me...

If you don't understand...

At least the books will...

And they won't judge...

They won't pressurize

And I'll be me...

Let me do what I'm good at...

Don't... please... don't make me another dead wife...

I beg you...

Don't send me off to die...

68. No More Safe... No More Secure...

Every story begins with a person...
And the place it happened...
And it doesn't stop...
Until the whole event is narrated...
With gory details...
And I... I've this image...
Stuck at the back of my mind...
Where a woman was forced...
To do this and that...
And there are millions of faces...
That came popping up...
Some darker than the rest...
People say...
"It's because of women...
That rapes exist..."
And some others say...
"That marital rapes are culture of India..."
And then some random parents say...
"We don't feel sorry for...
What happened to her...
She's a bad person after all..."
And it triggers me down to marrow...
And I hate to say it...
But... once I felt safe in India...

Felt India had my back...
But now... look at the chaos...
Look at the daughters of India...
Rotting down to hell...
The hell that's filled with men...
It seems that none of us women...
Are afraid of hell...
Cause we see monsters let loose...
The Lady of Justice...
Licking their boots like a faithful dog...
And she... blinded and unbalanced...
By the power and colourful notes...
And it's shame... brutal shame...
No more safe... no more secure...
A dangerous simulation...
Where I'm trapped alone...
I... I don't feel safe at all...
And I'm sorry to all those wonderful women...
Who could've become someone worthy...
Someone progressed...
But shame on you... you disgusting world...
You let her rot... like a half-bitten fruit...

69. In Between Chaos...

It feels like I'm in chaos...
I middle of an ocean...
Unable to swim towards any shore...
Trapped and floating...
Trapped and drowning...
What used to save me...
Was my faith that I could make everyone happy...
The idea that everyone smiled...
Because of what I did for them...
Everything was fine...
Until things went astray...
Until all hell went loose...
The spirits came crashing in...
To the world that I thought belonged to the living...
Maybe I'm mad...
Maybe I'm going mad...
I cannot see the barrier...
The boundary between real and the imaginary...
And you tell me to trust you...
And hold your hand and walk...
But I'm more blind than I thought to be...
And here I'm stumbling over and over again...
And now... I can feel...
Your anger seeping in from your impatience...
You're tired of my stumbling on everything...

And you want to leave...

But seemed chained to me...

And I let you go...

Let you walk away...

Cause it's always better to do that...

To let you walk to your happiness..

Rather than to stumble you down to hell with me...

70. Puppet Childhood...

I was a puppet...
Once upon a time...
And they always asked me to sing...
Or to dance...
And when I never did...
They would compare me...
With those who did...
They always asked me to wear make-up...
Paint my burnt lips in cherry red...
And to paint my dull cheeks...
A rosy pink...
And they would ask me to wear glittering stones...
And go to places...
Where I don't even wanted to go in the first place...
And then when I refuse...
They compared me again...
Said I'm horrible...
Said I'm lazy...
Said I looked ugly from every single angle they watched...
And I did cry...
I won't lie...
Cause I always wanted to fit in...
Or at least that's what I was taught...
And I would dance to their tune...
With my glass slippers...

Stolen from Cinderella's shoe rack...
Until the day...
When those glass slippers broke...
And pierced my feet...
And then... I stopped...
But they never did...
But I stopped...
And I never cared...
For they could vanish with those criticisms for all it matters...
And I... I began writing...
And writing all my pain out...
Screaming silently out to the world...
And the world...
They clapped...
They said...
That they fell in love with my words...
And they told me...
My words meant something to them...
And I felt... happier...
I felt relieved...
When that huge burden of pleasing people...
Just shed off from me like old skin...
I started breathing... finally...
Like a baby out of a womb...
And it mattered to some...